Published by
Hybrid Global Publishing
333 E 14th Street
#3C
New York, NY 10003

Copyright © 2025 by Tracy Doyle

All rights reserved. No part of this book may be reproduced or transmitted in any form or by any means, electronic or mechanical, including photocopying, recording, or by any information storage and retrieval system, without the written permission of the Publisher, except where permitted by law.

Manufactured in the United States of America, or in
the United Kingdom when distributed elsewhere.

Doyle, Tracy
Life Storms Finding Your Clear Sky

Paperback Book ISBN: 978-1-938015-09-0
Hardcover ISBN: 978-1-938015-11-3
eBook ISBN: 978-1-938015-10-6

Library of Congress Control Number: 2024925111

Cover design by: Julia Kuris
Copyediting by: Keidi Keating, Susan Salley
Interior design by: Tamara Smith
Author photo by: Maggie Yurachek

www.tracydoyle.life

Are You Ready for Change?

Are you feeling emotionally disconnected, stuck in negative thinking, or as if you're struggling to maintain meaningful relationships?

Do you feel overwhelmed, unappreciated, misunderstood, and as though no matter what you do, it's never enough?

Are you unsure how to break free?

Would you like to learn how to recognize and redirect negative thinking so you can restore connection and fulfillment in your personal and professional relationships?

If so, you're in the right place. *Life Storms: Finding Your Clear Sky* **and the Aurora Method® was created to show you how.**

Acknowledgements

There are many people who've helped, believed in, supported, and loved me through this journey. And without them, I wouldn't be where I am today. Each one of them, regardless of whether they're still with me, has made this book possible.

To the love of my life, Laurie Powell, who's walked by my side and given me the courage and strength to get through every storm. Your belief in and love for me has given me purpose and the passion to do all that I do. I love you with all my heart.

To my Mam, Dorothy L. Doyle, who was, and still is, my inspiration. You taught me the values of resilience and perseverance in all areas of life and challenged me to rise above.

To my uncle, Tim Doyle, whose kindness, generosity, and measureless commitment to family provided me with the means to thrive. And to the love of his life, my aunt, Anna Doyle, thank you for your guidance, nourishment, and wisdom. You gave me the ability to succeed in life, and your encouragement to tell my story gave me the courage to do it. I love you, and I'm forever grateful that God put you in my life.

A special thank you to my sister, Lisa Diane Bock, for finding me and being my lighthouse during my most recent storms. I'm grateful for your unwavering love and support. But I also thank my sisters, Sue Milewski and Diane Anton, and my brother, Bobby Ruscus, for welcoming me to the family and embracing me with your kindness and love. My cup is overflowing because of you. And to all my nieces, Lexie Anton, Allie Cibiniak, Katy Milewski, Rosie and Danielle Ruscus, Desiree Southgate, and Arieya Dolopei, and my nephew, Raymond Milewski, thank you for being who you are and letting me be your aunt and your friend!

To the Doyles, thank you for your love, your support, and most especially, for dancing and laughing with me! I love you.

I'm also blessed with beautiful friends who've walked with me on this journey. I'd like to thank Candace Kucy and Brenda Pateman for their commitment to helping me and their endless wisdom and life-changing support. I would also like to thank Donatella Graffino for your ongoing guidance, no matter where I am on the journey; Cindy Green for teaching me so many things, especially how to laugh; and Paul Mast and Chuck Vasquez for your years of friendship and encouragement, which gave me the inspiration to share my story.

Additionally, to all of you whose words of wisdom have helped me overcome the major and daily storms: Janet Hanna, Kathy Agnelli, Marti Caito, Tina Hansen, Missy Hennessy, Allison Kent, Lori Konig, Gwendolyn Monangai, Joan Scalera, Bonnie Scott, Fredi White, Trish Woods, and Kathy Yurkovich. And to my professional hero, mentor, and the leader whom I admire most, Marianne Smith. Thank you for giving me a chance. Your friendship and guidance propelled me to the next level. Also, shout out to Circle C for your professional wisdom that carried me through some of the toughest challenges in my career: Diana Galer, Tina Garyantes, and Marilyn Monda.

I'm filled with gratitude to our many clients who supported Phoenix, especially those who believed in us and supported our start-up: Kelley Jewett, Zandra Maffett Fennell, Barbara Felice, and Ron Jones. We're all forever grateful to you.

There aren't enough words to express my heartfelt thanks to Angela Fiordilino and every person who contributed to Phoenix and its success for over 20 years. It was the privilege of my lifetime to serve you. Although I struggled, and my storms may have made things difficult at times, your passion and innovation inspired and humbled me to strive to overcome my limitations. I'm very proud of each team member and the many achievements we've accomplished together. Thank you for all the success stories we've created, and most especially, thank you for your support. I'm forever grateful to have had the opportunity to work with you.

And finally, a special thanks to Keidi Keating, John Beausang, and Tamara Smith, whose support, encouragement, and expertise are indispensable. I couldn't have written this book without you.

Contents

Preface. xi

Introduction 1

Genesis 11

The Turbulent Twenties 33

Lost in the Tumultuous Sea 61

Eye of the Storm 83

Embracing the Waves of Change 109

Emerging from the Fog 129

Finding Your Clear Sky 155

Harnessing the Winds of Change 173

Clearing the Skies 187

Peering Above the Storm 203

Navigating the Turbulent Sky 223

Living in Your Clear Sky 233

Views for Your Life's Horizon 247

Let's Stay Connected 250

Resources 251

Additional Reading 271

Preface

I began my professional journey with a single purpose: helping others. I studied psychology and counseling, but life's circumstances took me in another direction. After a successful career in the pharmaceutical industry and founding and leading an award-winning, multimillion-dollar business, I felt called to return to that original purpose in a more personal way. I wanted to find a way to reach and help emotionally burned-out professional women who feel empty and alone reconnect with themselves and others in both their personal and professional relationships.

I didn't write this book because I had it all figured out. I wrote it because I didn't. I was that professional woman who managed it all. I may have looked put together on the outside, but inside, I was drowning in self-doubt, afraid I wasn't good enough, overwhelmed because I was doing it all myself, and angry because I never said no.

I felt like I was a human doing, not a human being. I didn't know how to be. Be okay with myself. Be content with my life. Be still. I thought that if I worked harder, stayed stronger, and continued forging ahead, it would get better. But it didn't. And I lost myself.

With the help of one friend, I found my way back. She showed me a framework to manage my thinking—thinking that affected everyone around me and held me back—that she'd learned from the book *Alcoholics Anonymous*. From this experience, I was able to piece together and apply everything I'd learned while studying psychology and seeking support to overcome childhood trauma.

Over the years, I've shared what I've learned with others and have been fortunate to be surrounded by a loving community of family and friends who've helped me build upon and refine my approach. The collective wisdom I've gained, coupled by my own studies and experience as a leader, friend, and mentor, inspired me to develop the Aurora Method.

The Aurora Method embodies the most meaningful insights I've gained on my journey. Its foundational practices are inspired by the work of several great psychologists whose contributions shaped the way we understand emotional healing, personal growth, and connection.

William James influenced my understanding of human experience. He taught that our beliefs matter. It's not just what we believe, but how our beliefs shape how we act. The idea that "truth is what works" when seeking to improve one's life motivated me to reflect upon how our life experiences shape our thinking and how our thinking affects our behavior in relationships.

Carl Jung's teachings about the interaction between the conscious and unconscious mind helped me understand the importance of bringing unresolved life experiences into conscious awareness. When there's a disconnect between the two, we remain stuck, limited by our thinking that cuts us off from ourselves and others. By shedding light on these unresolved life experiences, we can begin to set the process of change in motion.

Abraham Maslow's work deepened my understanding. He emphasized that unresolved emotional wounds—no matter when they occur—can disrupt the fulfillment of our core emotional needs for safety, love, belonging, and esteem. Where Jung helped me see the *why*, Maslow clarified the *what*: These unmet needs create the sense of inner emptiness and discontent that so many of us silently carry.

Lastly, M. Scott Peck taught that life's difficulties are not obstacles to growth; they're part of the path. His work helped me see that emotional and spiritual transformation begins when we stop avoiding painful truths and start accepting them. That insight became a core theme in my life: Acceptance is what allows us to navigate life's storms with clarity, resilience, and grace.

These teachings, as well as those that I'd gained from therapy, my friend, and self-help books written by authors such as Susan Jeffers, Don Miguel Ruiz, and Wayne Dyer, have *all* influenced the Aurora Method.

The Aurora Method is more than a process. It's a path to reconnecting with yourself and others. This step-by-step guided journey empowers you to improve communication challenges, manage emotional setbacks, and restore connection in your personal and professional relationships.

My goal from the start was to help others as so many have helped me. The Aurora Method is how I'm paying that forward—to honor those who stepped up when I needed them and be there for those who haven't had someone as their resilience champion. I'm here to help you recognize what's holding you back so that you can redirect your thinking and experience real, lasting change.

> "The greatest discovery of any generation is that a human can alter his life by altering his attitude."
>
> – William James

Introduction

We've all been wounded. We've all experienced some type of trauma. For many of us, these disturbing experiences occurred in early life, and they come in many forms and in varied degrees of severity. For some, it's being bullied by other kids or being criticized by parents or teachers. For others, it's emotional or physical abandonment by a parental figure; physical, sexual, or mental abuse; or trauma following a stressful event or physical injury. And many of us have experienced more than one.

Irrespective of the severity or the number of wounds, these experiences shape our thinking—our fundamental beliefs about ourselves and others. And navigating and breaking through the darkness of our life storms into a clear sky of healing is our life's journey.

The challenge is, how? How do we navigate?

My story is a journey of finding out how.

I was born into a large Irish Catholic family in New Jersey. Although I didn't know we were poor, I watched the family drink and dance, then laugh and fight. Big families come with their own complications but add alcoholism and the dynamics become chaotic: resentments build, emotions run high, and misunderstandings abound. My mother struggled with mental illness, but in a large, impoverished, alcoholic family, her condition was rarely acknowledged, let alone understood.

People with mental illness often battle with poor judgement and make bad choices that they're, sadly, unable to internalize and learn from. That was my mom. She struggled to be independent, and she repeatedly made poor choices. Some of those choices affected me profoundly.

I'd experienced the dark side of life by age eleven. I endured sexual, emotional, and physical abuse, along with the devastating effects of addiction. And amid it all, I was forced to take on the role of a parent, not only to my own mother but also to my two half-siblings. I desperately wanted out, and school was my respite and solution.

Survivor skills, anger, and intelligence were my strengths, and they helped me break free and get into college. I was the first in my family to attend and graduate. It was a big deal. I'd done it. I'd made it! But when I got out into the world, I was ill-equipped. The strengths that had gotten me there no longer worked in succeeding at life. Despite this, I was savvy and flourished in my career in the pharmaceutical industry. Then, I founded and built a multimillion-dollar medical communications company from the ground up, receiving numerous accolades and business awards. I'd made it out of poverty, and I was determined not to go back. But these accomplishments were merely who and what people saw. They didn't see the woman struggling inside.

I felt like I didn't belong. I was a scrappy street girl engaging with intelligent, well-to-do people with whom I had nothing in common. I didn't know how to fit in. I was embarrassed about where I came from and afraid of people knowing who I really was. I was smart and talented, but I didn't feel good enough. And at times, I felt outright unworthy. I struggled with relationships. I seemed at odds with people at work. I often felt misunderstood. I was frustrated and angry, and I felt sorry for myself.

Self-help became my go-to: therapy, workshops, the guidance of spiritual healers, and books. But in the process, I often found myself identifying with descriptions or characteristics of the problem. "Yes, that's me. I'm a trauma victim. I have imposter syndrome. What? I'm narcissistic too? Does that mean there's no hope?" Of course not. All I had to do was feel the fear and do it anyway, practice the Four Agreements, and manifest goodness. Got it.

But I didn't get it. I practiced and practiced. Then the practice faded, and when the struggles came back, I became stuck in my head and weighed down with labels, justifying and explaining why I did this and why I did that. It was everyone else who just needed to understand, but they didn't. It was a mindset that didn't work in my relationships nor in a leadership role at work.

I came to believe, and accept, that our life experiences *do* shape our thinking. They shape our attitudes about ourselves and others and what we do or don't do. Our experiences and our struggles, no matter what they are, build us into who we are, and most importantly, set us on a path toward who we'll become.

From my life experiences, I became a frustrated, insecure person who felt chronically misunderstood and needed constant validation. I became a person convinced that, no matter how good things seemed on the outside, I was meant to struggle on the inside. I believed that no matter how hard I tried, nothing would ever be easy. I was looking at life through a straw; I focused only on what I didn't have, rather than what I did.

By my mid-thirties, I reached a breaking point. My thinking affected all aspects of my life: my relationship with my partner, with my family, with my sense of well-being at work, and with my overall happiness. I was emotionally burned out.

I believed that the people around me and my circumstances needed to change. I didn't understand it was *my thinking* that needed to shift.

I'd gained many tools in therapy that helped with my life partner. My greatest gifts, however, were the everyday people in my life. Friends and family who had struggles and hardships just like me but found a clear path through the storms they called life.

They each had a sense of contentment, something I'd never had, and I wanted to understand how they found peace in their lives. Some went to church, while others only prayed. Some practiced meditation, while others practiced gratitude and manifesting abundance. Yet no matter what spiritual practices they adopted, they all had one thing in common: They were working to overcome the negative thinking that limited their lives.

The solution was mindfulness, and they each had a different approach to achieving it.

I learned that to overcome emotional burnout and break through negative thinking, I had to change my perspective and find my own mindfulness practice. I had plenty of people in my life offering their opinions, saying things like, "You shouldn't feel that way," or "Just let it go." But I didn't know how. And I certainly didn't know how to change my perspective and find my own way.

Over time, I came to understand that self-centered thinking was the problem.

A friend shared a self-assessment tool with me that she said would help me see that the problem was within me and not a result of anyone else. Of course, initially, I resisted. No one wants to accept that they're holding themselves back at best and outright hindering themselves at worst. But my friend said, "If nothing changes, then nothing is going to change."

The process wasn't inherently difficult. I just needed to open my mind and take the time and effort to do it. And when I finally did, I learned that it's not the actions or decisions of others or the hurdles thrown in our path that can take us down. It's our own thinking that distorts the way we see ourselves in the world around us.

Through deep reflection and the help of my friend, I uncovered how my life experiences created two foundational beliefs that, when triggered, ignited fear and drove my thinking and behavior.

My problem wasn't caused by the people or circumstances in my life—*it was within me.*

Self-centered thinking is a high-speed, one-way ticket into an enclosed city of limitation. It's not our experiences that hold us back but the way we internalize and respond to them. Finding my clear sky started with self-assessment (and became the impetus for The Aurora Method). I had to stop blaming, explaining, and justifying and become honest with myself about the role I played in creating my own barriers. That was a hard truth but one that gave me hope.

I was able to see and understand my behavior in the presence of fear. I knew what to change and had a path forward for how to change. All the books and tools I'd used over the years started to come together and make sense in an entirely new way because I had a better understanding of when and how to apply them. Things started to improve for me at home, with my family, and at work. It wasn't a perfectly smooth transition. I still had setbacks, mostly at work. But with guidance, practical tools, and mindfulness techniques, I was empowered to overcome them.

Applying the practices I've learned is what I call the Aurora Method, named after the Greek goddess symbolizing dawn or new beginning. And I'm an example that no matter where you've started in life, no matter what challenges you've faced, and no matter what traumas or wounds you've experienced, you can make a new start.

Everyday people can help everyday people, and I want to share what has been freely shared with me. I'm not a therapist. I'm merely a resilient professional woman who's endured trauma and emotional wounds that resulted in self-centered thinking and fears. I've broken through the limitations and misery they created for me and have realized personal and professional contentment. I'm an everyday person who has been helped by other everyday people who, like me, wanted meaningful relationships and a sense of purpose in their lives.

Eleanor Roosevelt once said, "No one can make you feel inferior without your consent." If you're struggling with communication challenges or unhappy because you feel unheard, misunderstood, or unappreciated by the people in your life, the Aurora Method may help you move toward the connection and fulfillment you've been longing for. You deserve to realize your own potential. You're worth the steps necessary to pave the way toward the version of yourself that trusts in and is empowered by what is possible tomorrow.

If you're struggling to feel connected and feel stuck or unsure about how to attain it, the Aurora Method may advance you toward it.

Throughout this book, we'll brave leaving the eye of the storm for the open skies of emotional healing and self-acceptance. I'll share the life experiences which shaped my thinking and show you how my thinking led me to emotional burnout. Then, we'll explore what I learned about self-centeredness and how these revelations propelled me to want to break free.

We'll explore how to navigate life's daily storms and practice a way of life that brings real and lasting change.

To live life is to face our experiences, good and bad. There's no one-size-fits-all solution. You won't be given a magical fix or a single 'secret' ingredient. Instead, you'll be introduced to the Aurora Method along with worksheets and exercises you can download. I'll guide you through them so that you can begin to apply the practices to your own life. We'll learn to be patient with ourselves and acknowledge our past choices. Through these activities, we'll step outside the fog to see our thoughts more clearly and piece together an actionable framework for growth—your personal plan—designed to create lasting, positive changes and help you step into the shoes of the person you want to be.

My experiences and the lessons I offer aren't a substitute for professional mental health support. Instead, they're meant to complement your overall mental health and wellness plan, reinforcing the care and expertise provided by trained professionals.

Healing and change aren't about what other people want or expect from you. They're about what you want for *yourself*, something you can only discover once you've climbed out of the torrent and can peer up into the clear blue sky. Don't let your thinking convince you that the sun no longer exists when it's waiting for you just above the clouds.

 Important Note: Trigger Warning

Before we begin, bear in mind that we'll explore potentially triggering topics such as childhood sexual abuse and traumatic events. While these topics won't be explained in detail, nor glorified, they will be discussed, as such experiences were a part of what shaped my thinking.

While my experiences may seem severe, try to identify with the feelings and beliefs that were shaped by them and avoid comparing your experiences to mine. And remember, we've all been wounded.

I hope that in sharing my own story, you can find comfort in the knowledge that you aren't alone, and that, regardless of the hurdles that've been tossed onto your path, you can break through your limiting beliefs and rise above each of them.

If you need to, please seek help from a mental health professional.

In the event you're grappling with trauma, or your mental health is hindering your ability to function in your daily life, I urge you to seek guidance from trusted, trained professionals.

Take breaks when you need them.

If you, at any point, become overwhelmed while reading, take a mindful break. Healing isn't possible if we inappropriately push beyond our limits into a further state of detriment. Take a breath, stretch, or participate in trusted rituals that calm and ground you, then return to this book once you're ready.

Genesis

I created a storm when I arrived.

When my mother's water broke, my grandmother thought some catastrophic health problem was occurring and rushed my mother to the hospital. She had no idea that this "crisis" was the birth of a six-pound, blonde-haired and blue-eyed baby girl.

I can only imagine my grandmother's shock. "Jesus Christ! What in the hell am I going to do?"

You see, my grandmother, Dorothy Doyle, whom I affectionately called 'Mam', was thirty-nine years old. Mam came from an educated and successful family in Somerset, Pennsylvania, and was swept off her feet by my handsome grandfather, Gus—whom I called 'Pop'. He was originally from Perth Amboy, New Jersey, a place where his large Irish Catholic family emigrated to in the 1800s.

Sadly, at the age of four, Pop lost both of his parents and most of his aunts and uncles to the flu pandemic of 1918. He and his siblings became orphans, and Pop and his brother were sent to Pennsylvania and raised in an orphanage there. Years later, Pop became a chef in the army, and when he returned to Pennsylvania, he and Mam married.

My mother was the first of their nine children. My grandparents eventually left Pennsylvania and purchased a home in Perth Amboy, New Jersey. Pop had become an alcoholic, and his addiction took Mam to the depths of despair. They lost everything—their home and their children. And faced with being homeless, my grandmother had to make hard choices. She temporarily placed all their children into an orphanage; some remained together, while others were separated.

Mam was forced to work during a time in our country when it wasn't socially acceptable for a woman to do so. In fact, it was a social stigma. But she was a survivor. She worked hard to rebuild her life and family. She and Pop moved to the port of Elizabeth, New Jersey, which was (and still is) a very poor section of the city. But eventually, Mam managed to bring their children back home, one by one—though, as you may well imagine, being chosen to be brought home over another sibling created deep and lasting wounds in each of my aunts and uncles.

Over a period of ten years, my family regained their footing. They moved to another location within the port, and as the oldest of their children, my mother bore the responsibility of caring for her younger siblings when Mam became the chief financial provider. But it was a responsibility my mom couldn't manage.

Back then, there wasn't a diagnosis for bipolar disorder, a mental illness that severely impacted my mom's daily life. One characteristic of bipolar disorder, especially in the teen years, is hypersexuality (being sexually impulsive and engaging in sexual activities frequently). My mother fit that description to a T, though without my grandparents' knowledge. Mam was unaware she was having sex in the house when she was supposed to be minding her siblings.

At eighteen, my mom became pregnant with me, but she hid it. According to my family, she'd always been chunky around the middle, and she wore a girdle, making the pregnancy less noticeable.

With no means to care for me when I arrived, my mother created a storm. She didn't reveal who my father was, and my grandmother was faced with raising another child—her first grandchild—together with my aunts and uncles, ranging from the age of four to nineteen.

That's how I was raised, more or less, as the youngest of ten children. I lived with my grandparents for the first few years of my life. My four youngest aunts and uncles who were closer to my age were more like siblings, whereas the other four who were closer in age to my mom were more like aunts and uncles.

I loved my family, especially Pop. He was a tall man with gray hair and a big belly. Pop was like Santa Claus. His blue eyes twinkled when he smiled, and he was very kind. He would hold my hand on walks, and we would go on excursions on the bus. When I was sleepy, he would let me nuzzle his belly and nap. Pop was my protector, and I felt safe with him, happily oblivious to his struggles with alcoholism.

Mam did her best to transition my mother to independence. Since my mom was unwed, my grandmother wanted her to live on her own, work, and raise me herself. Unfortunately, as a woman with mental illness, my mom didn't have the capacity to do it—she was unable to work and be a mother at the same time. It was too much for her. She tended to make poor decisions and bad choices, one of which was leaving me home alone as a toddler for hours at a time while she worked.

I recall waking from a nap when I was very young and being all alone. I walked around the house, calling for my mom. I hid in the closet until she eventually came home. When Mam learned that was happening, she was distraught, and plans were put in place to avoid it happening again.

My Aunt Pam started coming over to babysit me after school, then at another point, Aunt Betty moved in with us.

Aunt Betty was very affectionate. She showered me with gifts and playtime. She was fun, and I loved spending time with her. When Aunt Betty eventually moved out, though, we seemed to shift around, often going back and forth between living on our own or with my grandparents. I was too young to understand why we moved so much, and I certainly didn't understand what the yelling between my mom and Mam was about.

Four of my mother's siblings had successfully transitioned to independence. Three were married, and one went into the Air Force. With the remaining four children at home, my grandparents moved to a different section of Elizabeth into a third-floor, three-bedroom apartment, where my mom and I relocated with them. I was put in the room with my two aunts, and my mom slept on the sofa bed in the living room. We lived there until she got married.

That wasn't to say that life with my grandparents was perfect. My family struggled financially, but I didn't understand that we were poor and always felt secure when we lived with Mam and Pop. Having grown up in the Great Depression, my grandparents were incredibly resourceful. We ate a casserole of canned spaghetti and a box of Rice Krispies we called 'Hush Flush'. It fed us all. Sugar bread—white bread with margarine and sugar sprinkled on top—was often our dessert. We even made our own potato chips. It wasn't about survival to me, though. It was fun, and I loved making things with Pop. We had family dinner together every night, so it was easy for my young mind to not recognize the signs of our poverty.

My younger aunts and uncles were teenagers at that point, and my love for music was influenced by each of them. Uncle Tim would jam to the Allman Brothers or Grand Funk Railroad, and my Aunt Pat would sing along to America. We all loved Motown music. My other aunts and uncles and their spouses would come over for regular weekend celebrations. Everyone drank. Some played card games in the kitchen. And the rest of us played music and danced all night in the dining room. It was a great time!

Until it wasn't.

As a child, I didn't understand alcoholism. I merely learned the behaviors of my various family members, with no healthier concepts to compare them to, so when the weekend fights would break out, I accepted them. It's just how it was. Uncle Tim often comforted me during those feuds and showed me that silence and walking away protected us from getting hurt. But that also meant I accepted other behaviors far worse than excessive drinking which I was subjected to as well, all because I was too young to understand they were wrong.

Around the age of five, my eldest uncle started molesting me. He was handsome and had a great singing voice. He sang for us all the time, and I adored him. He was married, and periodically, he and his wife would invite me to their home for an overnight with them and their baby. But during those sleepovers, I would sometimes wake in the middle of the night to find him doing 'his thing.' I didn't speak up about it. I didn't know what to do. And he wasn't the only man who sexually abused me.

Our neighborhood was full of kids. There was one girl my age, and she became my bestie. She had an elderly uncle who lived with her family. He would sit on the porch all day and people-watch. He seemed very lonely, and we felt sorry for him. Sometimes, we would sit on the porch with him and eat treats and drink lemonade. We acted silly or would tell him jokes to make him laugh, and he seemed to enjoy our company. He seemed to be a very kind old man.

Until one day when I called on my friend to play, and her uncle was sitting in his usual spot on the porch. He told me that she and the family were away, and he asked me to stay and visit with him. I trusted him, so when he invited me into the house to get some lemonade, I had no reason to be afraid. But once we were behind closed doors, he forced me to perform a sexual act on him, and I couldn't understand what I'd done to cause that to happen.

Shortly after, while playing hide and seek with my youngest uncle and some of the boys from the neighborhood, one of the boys—who was around thirteen—lured me to an empty train car and raped me.

Those experiences led me to develop a strong belief that men were inherently bad and that they couldn't be trusted, because they would inevitably go out of their way to hurt me. And, over time, as the abuse continued, I started to believe I was somehow doing something to 'earn' it. While my grandparents and mother worked, my then seventeen-year-old Aunt Pat bore the responsibility of taking care of me and her two younger brothers after school. But she was often distracted by her boyfriend, so we spent most of our time outside.

Growing up on the streets of Elizabeth meant one had to have resilience and strength, and I quickly learned that if I was to go outside and 'play', I had to protect myself and those I cared about. Bullies were abundant, and they preyed on the weak, especially those who were younger and smaller. Although I was indeed small, I was also strong, and I became adept at successfully fighting to protect myself and my friends.

I was almost seven when my mother married. We moved from Elizabeth to a sunny apartment in Woodbridge, New Jersey, and our first year together was bliss. I had my own room, nice clothes, and my own record player. I loved to listen to the Jackson 5 and the Monkees while dancing and singing. The girl living in the building next to ours became my best friend, and since our buildings were close, we could talk to one another from our bedroom windows. We loved spending time together at each other's apartments and being out and about playing. I liked my first- and second-grade teachers and the kids at school. There was no need to fight anymore. Yes, for that first year, life was good.

My sister, Lisa, was born a few months after the wedding. She looked like an angel, with curly locks and rosy cheeks. I was so happy to have a baby sister, and my mom seemed to be on an entirely different footing. She didn't work anymore, so she was home and took care of us. And while, overall, she wasn't a very affectionate person, during this time in my life, she was. We played games, and I was her helper with the baby, preparing meals, and cleaning up.

Shortly after their first anniversary, however, things began to change, and dark clouds started to settle in.

My stepfather was a Vietnam War veteran. He was a skilled mechanic and a great provider. During our first year together, we never went without. He would come home after work, and we spent time together as a family. On weekends, there was always something to do—fishing, crabbing, or visiting his or our family. He had a large family too, and they would all gather on Sundays. We would eat, play games, then watch a movie. There were so many people but limited seating, so I never thought much about being told to sit on the floor to eat or watch TV.

The first change I noticed after that initial year was my stepfather no longer coming home after work. We often ate dinner without him. And when he did finally arrive, he would be in a drunken stupor.

My mom was pregnant with their second child, my brother Bo. One night, when he arrived home drunk, my mom yelled at him. Intoxicated and furious, my stepfather stormed right back out of our second-floor apartment—and fell down the flight of stairs. He crashed through the full-length glass door at the front entrance of our building. He was rushed to the hospital and returned home with a broken jaw.

One would think he would stop drinking after that, but he didn't. My stepfather was an alcoholic, and his alcoholism was progressing.

Because of my family, I'd had experience being around people who drank; they laughed, played cards, danced, and in most cases, got upset and fought. It was chaotic but predictable. In contrast, the kids on the streets were unpredictable and much scarier. But being engulfed in my stepfather's addiction was unlike everything I'd experienced before.

After my brother was born, we left what I perceived as an idyllic world. I no longer felt safe and secure.

I started third grade when we moved into the gray, ominous house. It was rundown and looked haunted, and I instantly felt uneasy. We were surrounded by woods and fields, and the other families in the neighborhood were poor. We were in what felt like a rural ghetto.

Although our yard was relatively private because of the surrounding trees, the forest felt as scary as the house. The only beauty was in the pussy willow and magnolia trees that had the most stunning blooms in the spring. Most of the kids in our neighborhood were much older than me, so I played outside by myself after school. It was very lonely, though I loved climbing the magnolia tree and sitting on a branch near the top. It was my happy place.

Up the street was the Maple Tree Tavern, the local spot for food, entertainment, and drink, and down the street and to the right was where my stepfather's parents lived. Since I didn't have anyone to play with, and I missed our previous neighborhood, I would sometimes visit my stepfather's mother, who everyone called Nanny. She'd always seemed nice, but I learned she was nothing of the sort.

During my first visit, she said, "Do you know why you're a little bastard?" When I said no, she replied with, "Because your mother is a whore, and you don't have a father! I don't know what my son sees in that whore you call 'mommy.'" She quoted scripture and said something to the effect of, "A bastard shall not enter into the congregation of the Lord," followed by, "You're not wanted here. Bastards aren't welcomed in this house."

I was eight years old.

That was the first time I felt different and unwanted. Before then, I'd never questioned why I didn't have a dad, because Pop was everyone's father.

I left Nanny's house and went home to ask my mother about it, but all she said was that he'd died in a car accident. But the truth was, I was an illegitimate child. A child born out of wedlock, and I wasn't accepted because of it.

I endured taunts from my stepfather's nieces and nephews when we would play during visits. Though once, when one of them pushed me too far with incessant name calling, since I was a street-smart kid who knew how to fight, I threw a rock and knocked his tooth out.

Nanny continued her denigrating behavior and said I was a devil child. She would prepare my plate and say, "Now, you little bastard, you sit on the floor and eat." If I tried to sit on any of the furniture, she would say, "Oh no, bastards sit on the floor."

I eventually looked up the word in the dictionary, but the definition confused me.

Was that why Nanny made me sit on the floor? Because being fatherless meant I was a dog? I couldn't understand why she was so mean.

I began to believe that I didn't belong, and after repeated taunts and cruelty, I concluded that I would *never* belong. I struggled with the idea that I had no immediate family that I truly belonged to. My stepfather wasn't my true dad; he was just a man my mother married. Their children weren't my brother and sister; they were only partially related to me. My aunts and uncles weren't my immediate family; they were my mother's. I grappled with these beliefs, and as I watched Nanny dote on her other grandchildren while treating me with disdain, I realized that being fatherless meant I wasn't good enough or worthy of being accepted.

Mam and Pop and the rest of our family seemed so far away.

My stepfather's addiction continued to progress, and things further deteriorated. He was more or less always intoxicated. He would leave for work in the morning and be gone all day and night, so he must have been working hard, I thought. Though I couldn't understand with all that work why we barely had enough to eat, and at times, why our lights and water didn't work, or why our clothes were never cleaned.

Over time, my mom became disengaged and played solitaire on the sofa all day. She would barely acknowledge me when I came home from school, and she began neglecting the kids.

I had to manage my schoolwork, take care of my sister and brother, and clean the house while dealing with my mother's unchecked bipolar rages, which became more frequent from the stress of my stepfather's drinking. She would become frustrated when I didn't understand my homework, would grab my hair and pound my head onto the table yelling, "What will it take for you to get it?" When I tried to be loving, she would pick me up by my hair and throw me into a wall, demanding I get out of her way. Other times, when we misbehaved, she threw shoes or beat us with them, and when we didn't have anything for dinner, she would throw pots, plates, and glasses all over the kitchen.

My mother was blinded by an all-consuming concoction of emotions she couldn't control, but that doesn't excuse her behavior. She was a small woman who became a huge monster to us.

I continued to find solace in the magnolia tree in our yard. I'd climb it every day and then go exploring and play with my imaginary friends in the woods. They helped me through the hardship and struggles. With them, I belonged.

My mother stopped taking care of us entirely when she eventually went back to work.

Faced with unpaid bills and no food, my mom secured a part-time job at night. And as the eldest child, I became the full-time caregiver by age ten. My stepfather would leave his job, pick up my mom, and drive her to work. I was often left home to fend for myself and the kids, with little or nothing to prepare for dinner. Sometimes my stepfather would return home and take us out to a fast-food restaurant, but he would often be so intoxicated that he'd make me drive his car with the two toddlers in the back seat. I sat on his lap, and he accelerated while I steered. I was terrified. Other times, he would bring home a bar pizza from the Maple Tree hours later. Although most of the time, he never came home, and we just didn't eat.

Despite both parents working, we didn't have enough money to pay our bills and put food on the table because of his drinking and, as we later learned, gambling. There was a small store across the street from my school where the owners could see how undernourished I was and would sometimes offer me sandwiches and other snacks to bring home, but food wasn't the only thing we were lacking. We couldn't afford electricity or running water, and our general lack of cleanliness resulted in lice and rotting teeth.

School became my respite from the insanity and chaos at home.

I didn't know how to handle crying children telling me they were hungry, so I just rubbed their bellies and backs and consoled them to sleep. I couldn't understand how my mother ignored their wails.

Nobody cares, I thought.

Over time, I resorted to racing kids in the schoolyard for their food, and if they lost but refused to hand over their lunch, I'd beat them up and take it. My rough-around-the-edges attitude wasn't for kicks; it was about survival and my obligation to look after my siblings.

I often prayed to God to take us out of the situation and for Pop and Mam to rescue me again. But they didn't come. Instead, occasionally, my sexually abusive uncle and his wife would invite me for the weekend or a week in the summer, and I always accepted. I jumped at the opportunity to get a bath and three good meals, despite knowing what was going to happen.

The abuse progressed from oral to penetration.

Over time, my prayers shifted to begging God to make my stepfather go away. He was the cause of all our problems, after all. Then I started wishing he would die. I didn't care how. I just wanted him out of our lives forever, sure that it would make everything better. That we would no longer be poor or dirty, and that I would never again have to hand myself over to my abusive uncle just to escape the torment that had become our life.

I'm not sure I expected my prayers to be answered, and I certainly didn't expect it to happen the way it did.

A few weeks after my eleventh birthday, I came home from school to find Mam at our house. Finally! But she and my mom were speaking in very serious tones, and they told me to go back outside. Later, when Mam was leaving, I overheard her say, "Go pack up some things for you and the kids, and I'll be back to get you tomorrow." Words can't describe the relief that flooded me. After four years of suffering, we were leaving hell.

We'd been living in complete squalor for more than a year. Filthy clothes were all over the floor in every room, garbage lay everywhere, dirty dishes filled the sink, and no running water also meant an unflushed toilet and disgusting scents permeating the air.

Our last evening with him followed the usual routine. My stepfather came home drunk, picked my mom up, and took her to work. During that time, the water and electricity were back on for a little while, and I found a half a loaf of white bread, some cheese, and a bit of milk in the fridge; Mam must've bought them. I made us dinner and put my siblings to bed in our parents' room after some TV. I stayed in the living room to stand vigil over the front door, so I collected my blanket and pillow and settled in on the couch for the night.

I awoke to my mother crying outside. She rarely drank, and when she did, she never got drunk, yet both she and my stepfather were intoxicated. He helped her into the house, and she sat on the floor, leaning onto the couch where I lay. She wailed and said, "I'm so sorry. I didn't mean for this to happen. Please forgive me," repeatedly. He just stood there, swaying with a bar pizza in hand. It was after midnight, but he was so out of it that he thought it was still dinner time.

The anger welled up inside me. I was disgusted with him. The drunk who'd made my mother cry. The drunk who didn't care about his kids, who didn't care if we were safe or if we starved, who didn't care that we were dirty, who didn't care his mother treated me like a dog—who just didn't care.

I glared at him and screamed, "Look what you did to my mom! I fucking hate you!"

He dropped the pizza on the coffee table and stormed into the kitchen and down to the basement.

Still crying, my mother got up with my help. I guided her to bed with my siblings, then crashed on the couch and pulled my blanket over my head, desperate to block out the world for just a few hours.

Part way through the night, I woke to loud clanging: *bang, bang, bang*. Then a strange moaning. I said to myself, "Oh my God, he's so drunk, he thinks he's fixing the furnace." I put my pillow over my head and rolled over to go back to sleep.

In the morning, my mother woke me. She asked if I knew where my stepfather was. I told her he went to the basement the night before, but when she opened the basement door from the kitchen and called his name, she got no response. Since his car was still parked outside, she went out the front door and around the house to the external basement entrance, calling his name again. I thought little of it—until my mom let out a blood-curdling scream.

I bolted down the basement stairs, rounded the corner, and slammed into something.

There, strung up in the doorway with a rope around his neck, and looking down at me with a cold, empty stare, was my stepfather's body.

Horrified, I scrambled back, trying to rush away. I couldn't stand, I was shaking so hard, and I pulled myself up the stairs and back into the kitchen. There, I rocked and cried out, "No, God! No! I didn't mean it!"

Later, we learned it hadn't been a suicide. My stepfather's rock bottom had led to his murder.

I'd been right. With his death, everything did change. But not in the way I'd assumed it would.

When we returned to the house the next day to retrieve our belongings, the place had been ransacked and all our things destroyed.

I was traumatized.

·~∽❀∽·.

Back then, in the mid-1970s, children were seen and not heard. Although my mother received counseling and psychiatric care, there was no intervention for me, and my mom's mental illness, poor judgement, and bad choices affected me profoundly. I already didn't trust men, and I began to no longer trust women either. I felt ashamed of my prayers and unworthy of God. God was, after all, the only authority who seemed to listen to me, but I couldn't even trust myself to turn to him anymore. I was left to manage my trauma alone.

We moved back in with Mam and Pop who, by then, had successfully transitioned all their children to independence except for my youngest uncle, Gus, who was four years older than me. My family rallied and helped my grandparents buy a home in North Plainfield, New Jersey, where all seven of us lived.

I was enrolled in the fifth grade in the middle of the school year. I stopped talking and struggled to concentrate or comprehend anything. I just couldn't understand what was being taught anymore, which had never been a problem for me before. We were often asked to stand and answer questions in class, but I couldn't. The other kids laughed and gossiped about me, calling me stupid.

One day, a girl in the hall asked me if I'd heard about the new girl. Since I *was* the new girl, I pretended I didn't know who she was talking about, and she said that the "new girl" was a freak and an idiot because "she" didn't even know the basics like the alphabet or how to add and subtract.

I'd been through so much up to that point and couldn't relate to the senselessness of childhood gossip. I struggled to fit in. Often struggling to or unable to speak, I focused on creative writing and art instead, and I discovered tennis.

My grandmother bought me a used bicycle and a tennis racket. I was thrilled. I would ride over to the grammar school and hit a tennis ball against the wall for hours. It helped me release some of my pain and anger. Other kids enjoyed it too, and since there was a line on the wall as if it were a net, we took turns. But the bully at school had also heard about me, and my used bike seemed to be her opportunity.

She was a short, burly girl with brown hair and a cropped Dorothy Hamill haircut. She carried herself like a muscled pro wrestler, which seemed to create a lot of fear with the other kids, but I was amused by her. She was nothing like the people on the streets of Elizabeth.

One day, while taking a break from hitting the ball, the bully approached and started making fun of my bike. She called me names, then jumped on my bicycle and rode it toward the wall. She leaped off before it crashed. She drove it into the wall a few more times before I calmly told her that she was making a mistake if she continued, but she wouldn't listen. So, I went to her bicycle and tossed it against the wall. Multiple times. She tried to stop me, to shove me to the ground, but I had a good footing and didn't budge. And when I shifted in her direction, the bully took off, scared of what I might do to her.

I learned that day that anger is power.

Suddenly, the other kids took an interest in me. I was no longer called "stupid" behind my back, and I eventually made friends, got involved in recreational sports and community organizations, and thrived in school and became the class president.

Around fourteen, my friends started dabbling with alcohol and marijuana, and at first, I was reluctant to try them, given my experiences with my family. But I eventually caved to the pressure and discovered smoking pot made it easier to fit in. I talked more, and the people around me considered me funny while buzzed or high. We became known as the "partiers" in high school.

I dated a boy who wasn't from my high school when I was in tenth grade. He was British and had a David Bowie vibe. His parents were very fond of me and embraced me as part of their family. I joined them on several outings, and they showed me another side of life that I'd never dreamed of experiencing.

He was soft-spoken, loving, and kind, and my trust grew deeper with him over time. One evening while cuddling, I told him about finding my stepfather's body and the sexual abuse I'd endured. He was the first person I'd told; I felt safe with him. He hugged me and said, "I'm so sorry you went through that." He also mentioned that I might need help and encouraged me to tell my family.

It took a while before I finally followed his advice.

When I eventually had the courage to speak up about the sexual abuse, I first told my mother. I trembled as I spoke. She listened, but then asked, "What do you want me to do about it?" I instantly shut down, and in my head, I screamed, *"Be a mother and protect me!"* But when all I said out loud was, "I don't know," she told me to let her know when I "figured it out."

I felt overwhelmed and didn't know what to do. I stopped caring about my grades and continued smoking weed daily. I failed geometry that year and had to go to summer school.

A math teacher lived above my Aunt Ann and Uncle Tim's apartment, and they suggested I live with them for a few months during summer school, so I could get extra help. They were more like a brother and sister to me, and we'd always been close. I was happy to spend more time with them.

One night, we were talking about the uncle who'd molested me. They'd expressed dismay about something he'd done, and I blurted, "Oh, I know. You have *no idea*." But since I didn't know anything about the situation that they were talking about, my aunt looked bewildered and said, "What do you mean by that? What are you talking about?" That's when I finally mustered the courage to tell them about the abuse and how long it had gone on for.

They echoed what my boyfriend had said, that I needed help, and asked if I'd spoken to anyone else. I told them about the exchange with my mom—and since we didn't understand her mental illness yet—they were as upset as I was.

The next day, Aunt Ann said, "You need help, which means we have to tell the rest of the family, especially your grandparents." I was afraid, but my aunt said she and Uncle Tim would handle speaking with everyone and would figure out how to get help, so I reluctantly agreed. I trusted them.

The next day, Uncle Tim spoke to Aunt Dot who wholeheartedly believed me because, apparently, my uncle had molested his siblings as well. She took action right away and found a therapist.

Aunt Dot took me to weekly appointments, unbeknownst to my grandparents.

I hadn't been aware of when they'd planned to speak to my grandparents, so when I arrived home that day, I wasn't prepared for the wrath of both Pop and my mother. Apparently, the meeting was to be held at my aunt Betty's house. Uncle Tim, Aunt Ann, and Aunt Dot were to be present, but while they were enroute, Aunt Betty thought it best to tell my grandparents without them. My aunts and uncle were upset because she hadn't spoken to me directly, and they knew the details. No one truly knows what was communicated, and sadly, the news divided our family.

Mam was distraught and believed that my uncle was guilty. Pop, on the other hand, was upset and drinking and called me a liar. Meanwhile, my mother was angry, but only because I'd told Aunt Ann and Uncle Tim. She was furious that she wasn't the one to tell Pop and Mam. She scolded me for betraying her. She didn't understand that I never asked them to get involved. They were the ones who took charge as any healthy adult would upon learning about a child's sexual abuse.

I became the black sheep, no longer accepted by some and unloved by those that mattered to me. Nanny had been right: I was a bastard. I was unworthy of belonging.

Despite working through the abuse in therapy, I'd already internalized the mixed reactions of my family. I believed honesty wasn't worth the effort because it only caused division. Silence and isolation kept things intact. But I did learn at least one thing in therapy: I just had to get out. I needed to stay focused on school, get myself to college, and break free from it all—and never look back.

The Turbulent Twenties

Independence. Freedom from my mother. That was my aspiration as I transitioned into young adulthood. I saw myself getting my college degree, a good job, and meeting the person I would build a life with. I was optimistic and excited—until I hit some turbulence.

We all have people in our lives who teach us things on our journey that we may not understand at the time. For me, some people in my life created the storms, while others helped me navigate through them.

My Aunt Ann and Uncle Tim, eight years my senior, played a pivotal role in my life even before they learned about the abuse. They got married when they were sixteen and influenced me in many ways. When I was young, they were like my older brother and sister. My fondest memories are of spending summers with them, going to the beach in their convertible VW Beetle, learning how to cook or just hanging out, hearing my uncle's funny stories after work, and dancing in the kitchen while washing dishes. As I got older, though, they took on more of a parental role.

Mam, my grandmother, was my inspiration. Mam was hard-working, and she showed me that if you persevere, you can do anything. She would often say, "If you work hard and get a college education, you'll get a good-paying job, and then you can experience life." She spoke from long-fought-for experience gained after raising her nine children and earning her bachelor's degree while in her fifties. Mam was very proud when I went to college. I was the first of the children to go. Although she was unable to pay for my tuition, she challenged me to work hard for my education if I really wanted it. And like her, work hard I did.

When I transitioned to college, Mam wanted—and needed—me to be independent. She had already taken on the emotional and financial burden of caring for my grandfather, my mother, and my sister and brother. I recognized how hard those obligations were on her. She was doing her best to support us, and I didn't want to be a deeper burden on her than I'd already been. So I worked two or three jobs at a time to earn my degree. Since Mam was involved in helping the others in our family, I emotionally leaned on Aunt Ann and Uncle Tim.

I had a difficult start when I returned to college for my sophomore year.

I didn't own luggage; I only had plastic crates and green garbage bags. And that year, I had a new roommate, but I didn't think much of it as I claimed one of the small lockers which served as closets in our room. I unpacked my priority items first: my work clothes, a wardrobe I'd built piece by piece with my earnings since high school. But my suite mates were throwing a party, so I left the garbage bags with my casual wear and shoes next to my closet and enjoyed the festivities.

The next morning, my bags were missing.

When I asked my new roommate if she knew where they were, she said "Oh, I thought they were filled with trash, so I threw them down the chute last night." What? She had to be kidding, right? But she met my devastation with a devious smirk and tears welled in my eyes as she said, "Oh my God, I can't believe I did that!" and then called her friends and laughed about it all day.

I had to work that night but had no shoes, so I called my mom for help. But she offered no comfort. As I cried and told her what happened, she said, "What the fuck do you want me to do about it? Deal with it!"

Right, I said to myself, *nobody cares.*

I hung up and vowed to never call her again when I was in need.

Aunt Ann took the situation seriously when I reached out to her. We mapped out a plan of how I was going to replace everything over time. She said, "You'll be okay. You'll get through this," and told me to drive to their apartment. When I got there, she gave me two pairs of jeans, two shirts, and two pairs of shoes to get started. "See?" she said. "You've got enough."

That was a very difficult semester. I struggled emotionally because my roommate abused drugs and had no remorse for what she'd done. I was stuck reliving the same loss and loneliness I'd experienced with my stepfather. I again felt misunderstood, unloved, and unsupported by my mother, and despite multiple jobs, I struggled to afford food, books, and on-campus housing. I was beginning to feel hopeless.

I tried so hard, not wanting to let my grandmother down, but I didn't think I could do it. Maybe I wasn't as much like her as I'd believed. Maybe I couldn't be as strong and determined as her.

I convinced myself I wasn't capable of it. But I kept pushing. For her. My reflections on perseverance helped. Specifically, the quote by Winston Churchill, "Never, ever, ever, give up," because it spoke to the idea of never giving up in the face of overwhelming odds and to keep going. It was hard to keep going at times, because giving up seemed much easier.

My aunt and I spoke every day starting in my freshman year and into my sophomore year. Aunt Ann and Uncle Tim knew I was overwhelmed with attending classes, studying to get and maintain good grades, and to pay my way, so they eventually invited me to consider living with them to take a bit of the stress off my shoulders. They wanted me to succeed and knew I didn't have anyone else I could rely on.

I moved in with them after completing the first semester of my sophomore year. They lived in a modest two-bedroom apartment in Elizabeth, New Jersey, with their three daughters. They weren't financially well-off either and struggled to get by too, yet they welcomed me into their home and took care of me like I was one of their own children. They were determined to figure things out together, as long as I kept doing my part to improve myself. And for the first time in my short life, I felt like I belonged.

Up until that point, the only person I ever counted on and completely trusted had been Mam. I couldn't trust my mom; she was inconsistent and emotionally unavailable. After I endured sexual abuse by men whom I'd once trusted and betrayal by Pop, I believed men were inherently bad and you could not trust them. Uncle Tim, though, showed me that some men were kind and could be genuinely good and trustworthy, and Aunt Ann nourished and encouraged me. Whenever I was down and filled with self-doubt, she would say, "Snap out of it, little sister! YOU CAN DO THIS!"

My aunt and I would have deep and spiritually meaningful conversations as we sipped our morning tea and coffee. We had dinner together every night as a family, and my uncle would tell us about his day, sharing whatever struggle he may have had while helping us see the lesson in it all. He told silly jokes that made us laugh, and I watched him wrestle with my cousins.

On Tuesday nights after work, I would go to Game Night with Aunt Ann and her friends, and on weekends, I would hang out with them at home or at a friend's house. Though it didn't happen often, whenever we had the extra money, we'd go out together, and no matter where we were, we always danced.

I learned a lot from Aunt Ann and Uncle Tim. They taught me basic life skills; they taught me what a good relationship looked like and the importance of communicating honestly. And most importantly, they taught me the value of family and sticking together when things get tough. I watched them manage through personal hardships and loss. I watched them love and enjoy each other and their children. They were great parents, and on some level, I felt they were my parents too.

For once, my life truly felt stable and fulfilled. I was content when I was with them.

Their support helped me do well in college. I had a double major in psychology and counseling, and I consistently made the dean's list. I got involved with one of the college organizations and grew into a leadership position. I thrived and felt a sense of well-being and belonging.

But the turbulence kicked back in when I turned twenty-one, and Aunt Ann delivered these heavy words. "You must do this on your own now. It's time. You need to get your own place." At first, I felt rejected. What had I done wrong? My aunt must have sensed my fear, though, because she said, "You're ready. You can do it." She wasn't trying to get rid of me. She was trying to encourage and support my growth.

So, despite my anxiety, I figured out how. There was a house with two rooms and a shared bathroom in an attic across the street from my college. I rented half a room, and the journey to independence began.

I met a great guy at a college party, and after dating for some time, I thought he was the one. He was kind, loving, and cared for me like no other. He reminded me of Uncle Tim in some ways, and I wanted the kind of relationship my aunt and uncle demonstrated. We even talked about marriage. I wanted that traditional relationship, and I loved him dearly. But I didn't feel worthy of his love in return.

Even though I was dating a man, and I'd had a boyfriend before him, deep down, I always knew I was attracted to women. The feelings had started when I was in the sixth grade, but I'd pushed them down. Nobody in my family was gay, and my first exposure to a gay person was a guy I worked with while in college. I listened to his struggles about being accepted and dating, and the gay lifestyle seemed hard.

I didn't want to hurt my boyfriend, but after much heartache, I decided to break things off and finally allowed myself to explore my sexuality. When we separated, he was devastated and confused because we enjoyed one another, got along well, and loved and understood each other. Our families loved us as a couple too and hoped we would marry just as much as we had. I was ashamed to tell him and them the truth, but I couldn't lock either of us into a commitment that was dishonest.

Everyone was disappointed in me.

I'd met a beautiful woman in a class a year before the breakup. She had dark curly hair, warm brown eyes, and cinnamon skin, and she dressed fashionably. I was instantly struck the first day she walked into the room, and I made it my mission to talk to her with the intention of potentially gaining a friend, since at the time, I'd still been in denial with myself.

I approached her one day and invited her for a coffee, and we did indeed become fast friends. We talked daily, sometimes multiple times a day. And over time, we began talking about our relationships. She had a boyfriend as well, and her mother wanted her to marry him, a mirror to my situation.

We talked about what we liked about the men in our lives, but as we trusted each other more, we started to talk about how something was missing from our relationships. Something that we couldn't quite seem to identify. I soon learned that she was like me; she had feelings for women too.

My attraction to her had already been intense, even while I was still suppressing my sexuality. I'd never felt an attraction like that before, only crushes here and there. I eventually found the courage to come out to her, and she said that she felt the same about me.

As our attraction grew stronger, and our prior relationships ended, we decided to explore this part of ourselves further and became a couple.

Sadly, it wasn't a healthy introduction to embracing my true self. My coming-out journey was chaotic and tumultuous. I went from a kind, loving, caring relationship to an abusive one I hadn't seen coming.

The gentleness and trust I'd experienced before we jumped into a relationship quickly shifted. She constantly picked fights, and at times, our fights became physical. She was unstable, and it became clear that I'd made a bad choice. I was reliving the abusive relationship with my mother, and I needed to get out. I needed to regain my stability again, but I felt alone. I was afraid to tell the people who mattered most in my life that I was gay, and that the woman I'd left my ex-boyfriend to be with had been a mistake. I didn't know what to do. I couldn't see a way out of the situation.

I called the therapist who'd helped me tremendously in high school. His work was the catalyst for me having had a healthy relationship with a man. He'd guided me in many ways, and I trusted him, yet I was a bit apprehensive about coming out to him and seeking his help in this new way. I'll never forget our initial conversation when I went to see him again.

After listening intently, he said, "Okay. Well, if you're gay, we're going to make you the best damned lesbian out there!" I had hope.

We worked together for over a year, and he guided me to safely get out of that toxic relationship. I'm not sure what would have happened had it not been for his support.

I eventually met another woman and started the journey over, but this time, we had a healthy relationship, and I slowly regained confidence that it was possible to trust someone with my heart.

But instead of fearing my partner, I found myself filled with a different kind of fear and self-doubt. Becoming who I was meant to be was hard. I faced and walked through the fear of living on my own. I had roommates, but I was on my own, nevertheless. Although I accepted and overcame the fear of being true to myself, being gay created even more fear. I was afraid of being rejected by friends and family, especially by Mam, Aunt Ann, and Uncle Tim.

When I eventually had the courage to come out to them, they expressed disappointment, but they still accepted me. Although they, on some level, blamed the uncle who'd molested me, I knew I'd been born this way. My first same-sex crush had been in the second grade.

Out of love and concern, my family was afraid I would have a hard life without a man. What they didn't realize, however, was that their acceptance (despite their worries) gave me the strength and courage to live in my truth.

A friend's mom once said, "Life is a long, windy, twisty, bumpy road." At the time, I didn't fully grasp what that meant—but after graduating college, I began to understand. The path forward was never a straight line. There were detours, setbacks, and unexpected turns, but each one carried a lesson.

In addition to working part-time in retail during college, I held another part-time position as a residential counselor at a group home for the mentally ill. When I graduated, I was offered a full-time position there. I had big aspirations of becoming a clinical psychologist and a college professor. I wanted to go to NYU for my graduate degree. Unfortunately, I couldn't afford it on a counselor's salary, and I was in debt from my undergraduate degree.

I also couldn't afford to live and drive in the State of New Jersey because rent and car insurance were so expensive. I was living paycheck to paycheck. My friends were doing well financially, renting or buying on their own, but that wasn't possible for me. I couldn't reconcile the amount I owed for my undergraduate degree and the cost of my master's for a job that would only return a fraction of my investment, despite loving what I did.

My relationship had progressed positively, and we were ready for more. But given my financial situation, we needed a roommate despite wanting to live alone.

Faced with my first twist in the road a few years out of college, I had to make a choice: abandon my dream or apply my skills in some other way so I could achieve financial independence.

I was mentored by a co-worker who was a psychiatric nurse. She said my listening skills would take me far in business, but I couldn't see how. She encouraged me to apply my skills to the pharmaceutical industry, using her own experience in doing the same with her clinical skills as an example. I reflected on that and realized that if I was going to achieve independence, I had to adapt to my reality, abandon my dream, take the risk, and swim in my strengths.

She introduced me to a recruiter who frankly told me I needed to change everything about myself if I wanted to be considered for a job. And she meant *everything*: my hair, clothes, shoes, nails, purse, and briefcase. The only thing that could remain were my glasses! *Yikes,* I said to myself. *I can't afford that.* I felt ashamed, and the limiting beliefs raced around my head and convinced me that I couldn't do it and that I was destined to struggle for the rest of my life. Then I heard my aunt in my head saying, *Snap out of it, little sister!* I took a breath and said to the woman, "Thank you for the feedback. This is all new to me. I put myself through college, and I really don't know what to do. I'll do whatever you think is necessary." The recruiter liked my attitude.

I learned then that if I wanted to succeed in business, I had to learn not to take things personally. But at the time, I was embarrassed. I didn't know how to dress properly. I didn't know how to eat properly. I'd never had my nails done professionally. I didn't own a suit, let alone a briefcase, and I didn't know what a professional haircut or handbag was supposed to look like.

At first, her words felt like judgement and scorn, and I was ready for a street fight until I reminded myself that I'd gone to her specifically *for* her help. She was guiding me on what a professional appearance needed to look like. Through that experience, I learned that how I presented myself was the first step in breaking out of poverty. And if I was going to break free, I had to be open-minded and teachable.

I called Aunt Ann and told her everything the recruiter recommended. She said, "Okay. You need to learn. I'll help you." We went shopping together; my aunt and uncle were always there for me.

I was interviewed by two large and one small pharmaceutical company. I felt intimidated by the professionalism of the people who worked at the two larger ones. They were well-dressed and well-spoken. How could I ever measure up? I couldn't believe the compensation package I was offered by one of them, but ultimately, although it meant less money, I accepted the position with the small company because I thought it would make transitioning out of counseling to the business world easier.

Despite the smaller offer, I was over the moon. I'd nearly quadrupled my counseling salary. On top of that, I was given a company car with insurance and my gas paid for. I thanked God from the bottom of my heart, feeling like I'd already 'made it'.

My first week on the job demanded training in Boston, and I was thrilled to travel. I could count on one hand how many times I'd left New Jersey.

I was in a roomful of people who had different life experiences than me. I felt like a wallflower. They talked about their husbands, their fiancés, their kids, their vacations with friends and family, fashion, food, and so many other things I couldn't relate to. It was exciting but also terrifying, and I was gripped by fear and self-doubt.

How was I going to fit in? What could I talk about? I can't tell them about my life. What were they going to think? What if they found out that I'm gay? They would surely think I was an idiot once they figured out I didn't know anything about life. Who could I talk to? Could I even trust people in business?

My mind raced.

Since I was very observant and a good listener, after all, I realized I'd just needed to listen to each person and their stories. *Most people want to talk about themselves anyway,* I thought, and as a counselor, I was a one-way mirror. People often felt close to me. *I can do this.*

I observed how people dressed, how they ate, what wine they drank, and how they drank it—and I mimicked them. Through observation alone, I taught myself what to do.

Along the way, I met a woman from New England, and we became dear friends. When she was with me, and I was faced with a new experience in a formal setting where I didn't know the proper thing to do, she was aghast. But when I explained that I never learned, she was kind. She took the time to elevate my self-taught skills by showing me what to do. She guided me on many occasions, and she helped me overcome my shame and embarrassment by teaching me to laugh at myself.

It was a dramatic shift from counseling to pharmaceutical sales. While I'd been a counselor, my day had been structured for me, and I'd helped clients by actively listening and asking probing questions. I'd participated in clinical discussions with my supervisor. I'd felt like my contributions mattered. When I embarked on pharmaceutical sales, however, I had to structure my own day, navigate my way around cities and towns I was unfamiliar with, without tools like GPS or a cell phone. I had to earn a physician's trust before having a clinical discussion. And when I asked probing questions, I was either met with anger, "Who the hell do you think you are?" or disdain, "How dare you question me?"

My earlier life experiences that shaped and propelled me into getting my college education started to affect me in a much different way. I was engaging with physicians and people with advanced degrees. Their life experiences were truly a world apart from mine. Those people, in my mind, were better and smarter than me, and no matter how hard I tried to fake it until I made it, I didn't know how to belong in a world of smart and professional people.

I struggled during my first year. Sales is a lonely job. You're alone all day until you meet with a customer, and even then, physicians are skeptical of pharmaceutical sales representatives.

On one day, I met with a pulmonologist who seemed visibly annoyed by my presence. He was dismissive and became agitated when I asked him a probing question. In counseling, when someone exhibits behavior like that, the counselor points it out by saying, "You seem agitated with me." But in sales, that was a mistake. The doctor started throwing the samples of my product at me and called me horrible names. I'd worked with people who had severe mental illness and encountered aggressive behavior before, but that experience was unlike anything I'd dealt with professionally. I felt humiliated.

I believed then that I'd made a terrible mistake leaving my dreams and aspirations behind. I was sure I would never make it in the business world.

Eventually though, I found my respite. I drove to another physician's office and ended up telling them the story. We laughed together about it. Ah, connection!

Humor helped me overcome the self-doubt, and I worked hard at perfecting the art of telling funny observations during my visits with physicians. I became adept at embellishing an unusual encounter throughout my day. I made people laugh, and the laughter brought us together. And slowly, I began earning trust. My job took on more meaning.

I was a sales representative with a social worker's mentality. I sold an asthma product, and I worked in the inner city. As I gained trust and had meaningful discussions and discovered problems that needed to be solved, I found my purpose. I was on a mission to help underserved children with asthma and became a top performer. I grew to love my job and even won awards, trips, and extra bonuses. I was thrilled, but I didn't know how to handle that type of success, and I became unable to see outside of my microcosm. I lost interest in understanding differences and believed I had all the answers to successful selling, despite having no experience in other parts of the country.

My success blinded me and gave birth to self-importance. I was all that. I had arrived.

As I was recognized positively at work, I took it upon myself to be the voice of the underdog. I thought it was my duty as a successful person to call out others' grievances or point out injustices directly with my manager or corporate leadership. My head swelled, but I couldn't see it. I lost touch with myself, and while I was insecure on the inside, I was becoming arrogant to the rest of the world. And in my mind, justly so. I abandoned personal growth and my spiritual talks with friends and Aunt Ann.

The material world replaced my reflective, spiritual one, and I forgot my humble beginnings. My life was exhilarating. Who had time for reflection, anyway? I'd moved on from counseling, my relationship was going well, and my world was expanding beyond my high school and college friends and family.

There were three women from my company whom I adored. We enjoyed spending time together outside of work and traveling. There were a few doctors I developed great relationships with as well. One, who was from Italy, became a very dear friend. She educated me on worldly things. We had deep and meaningful conversations and lifted each other up when we were down. I felt very fortunate. I'd surrounded myself with great people who were trustworthy, professional, and fun, and they taught me so much about acting properly in business. But they also noticed my new habits and tried to coach me on how being the spokesperson for the underdog may not be a good idea for my career.

And they weren't the only people in my life who recognized the changes in me.

I don't know what prompted it, but during one of my regular calls with Aunt Ann, she told me that she'd liked me better when I'd been a counselor. I couldn't understand why. When I asked about it, she said, "I don't know. I just liked you better." She obviously saw something I didn't yet, something I was unwilling to acknowledge, even with the nudges of others. But unlike in the past, I didn't seek to understand what my aunt was trying to tell me. Instead, I dismissed it. I was clearly doing just fine, better than had ever been possible for me financially and professionally before.

I couldn't see the turbulent skies ahead.

From the outside, I was doing well. I was successful. I was receiving praise and awards for my work, and my relationship was going strong. Our friends loved us as a couple. We had a nice apartment and home life, and there was a lot of conviviality with our loved ones. We traveled; we laughed. We had fun. I felt like our relationship was akin to my aunt and uncle's.

On the inside, however, something was holding me back. I perfected being a one-way mirror at work and grew more insecure. I was afraid to be open about my lifestyle with my coworkers and clients for fear of losing my job. My partner was afraid too. And living in untruth ate away at my soul.

As a child, I'd developed the belief that I didn't belong, and as an adult, I felt similarly in the professional world, regardless of my efforts and the praise. *Maybe my aunt was right after all*, I thought to myself. *This life is going to be hard.*

I was living the lie, and life was getting more complex with my family. There was a lot of uncertainty and demand from them.

My sister Lisa was diagnosed with bipolar disorder later in life, but at the time, we just thought her behavior was bad. She often lied and started to steal; she became taxing on Mam. And without the knowledge of her mental health struggles, to me, Lisa's problem seemed to be related to losing her father and enduring my mother.

My mother, bipolar herself, was also ill-equipped to manage Lisa's behavior. She beat her daily. It was hard to watch her pound my sister's head. My grandparents worked, so they didn't see what was happening. I was afraid of my mother and therefore scared to 'tell' on her, though I did my best to console Lisa. When I'd left home to go to college, my sister took it hard. She destroyed or threw away what little I had from my childhood because my mother told my siblings that I'd abandoned them and didn't love them anymore.

Sadly, they'd believed her.

Mam retired when Lisa was eighteen, and someone stole her retirement gift money. She had put all the cards containing checks and money in a special purse in her bedroom as a safeguard before depositing the money in the bank. She discovered that the purse was missing and found it empty in Lisa's bedroom. My grandfather was ill, and my grandmother was distraught. Despite the evidence, Lisa denied taking the money, and since she lied often, Mam called me for help. She was going to kick my sister out of the house, and she thought Lisa could stay with me instead. But I was living in a healthy relationship and didn't want my family issues affecting it, so I refused to take Lisa in. I didn't trust her, and I made a healthy choice for myself, but I still felt like I'd let Mam down.

My grandfather died shortly after.

Pop had been diagnosed with lung cancer, and his passing struck me hard. I grew up with him and loved him deeply. We'd spent a lot of time together and had been very close when I was young. He'd talked to me a lot about life and shared his wisdom.

My grandfather had wanted to be a priest, but he stuttered and was rejected by the Catholic Church. Despite how hurt he was, he always said that God loved us all and that the church was an institution created to instill law and order in society at a time when it had been needed. We practiced Catholic traditions, and he taught us the teachings of Jesus.

Having grown up as an orphan during the Great Depression, Pop told us many stories about it. He'd consistently stressed the importance of being grateful for what we had and accepting others and practicing kindness. Which was all the more reason why I was devastated when he didn't believe I'd been molested. I felt betrayed by him. He was my Pop, my protector, yet he looked at me as a liar and an enemy of the family. So, I did what I knew how to: I distanced myself from him for almost ten years. I took for granted that he would always be around.

Pop got sober before he died. He once invited me to meet him out for lunch because he wanted to talk to me. Though I struggled to reconcile that forgiveness meant letting go of hurt, I agreed to see him. During our meal, he made amends as part of his recovery process, and it was the most beautiful experience. He said that he knew all along that my uncle was a 'bad seed' and was very sorry that he said and acted like he didn't believe me. He said that he didn't want to deal with the harms his son created and now understood how hurtful that was. He told me he loved me very much and was sad that he was not able to protect me. What he said helped me finally forgive him and, most importantly, heal our relationship.

I was by his bedside the night before he died. Pop was a big loss for me. I'd missed ten years with him because of alcoholism and the resentment it had created.

Grieving was difficult because of the chaos with Lisa. I don't know how my grandmother managed it all.

A few months before Pop died, Lisa claimed she'd been gang raped, but the police thought she was fabricating the story. My mother believed Lisa and was angry that nobody believed her, especially me, since half of our family didn't believe my own experience with sexual abuse. But Lisa lied so often, how were any of us expected to take her at her word?

Two weeks after the alleged incident, my mom called to tell me that Lisa had been telling the truth; she was twelve weeks pregnant. "This is preposterous!" I said. "How could she be that far along if she was raped only two weeks ago?" My mom wasn't able to make the connection.

That was the type of complexity we faced with my mentally ill mother and sister. Big lies, the inability to differentiate the truth from delusion, great financial need, and the inability to have a sound, responsible discussion without a fight. It was pure chaos, and the stress it caused my grieving grandmother was immense. She no longer wanted the responsibility and burden. She wanted to retire. She'd had dreams of traveling with her husband, and they were shattered.

My mother had a lot of resentment toward Mam. She said mean and unkind things about her and tried to turn us against her. I struggled with that because I regarded my grandmother as our savior. Without her, where would we be? She was reliable. Trustworthy. Our provider. She loved and valued our family. She'd sacrificed herself for all of us. She was my role model.

Mam wanted Lisa to give the baby up for adoption. My mother's reaction was intense. I couldn't understand the depth of it. At one point, she yelled, "She's not going to do to her what she did to me!" What? Stunned, I asked my mom what she was talking about, but all she said was, "Nothing."

My mother couldn't care for her grandchild. She couldn't even raise her own children and lived with her own mother for most of her life. Instead, she wanted herself, Lisa, and her grandchild to live with her retired, grieving mother, believing that either Mam or I should support them. And if we didn't, we were selfish, cruel, and only cared about money. They didn't have the capacity to understand the strain they created from their hypersexual behavior and bad choices.

My grandmother always made the difficult decisions.

Lisa and her son went to a shelter, and Lisa was arrested two weeks later with two men in a stolen car. Her baby was taken from her and put in foster care. She later went on to have another child with a different man, and she managed to regain custody of her son, but by then, she'd been estranged from us for nearly three years.

After dealing with this dilemma, Mam lost her youngest son, my uncle Gus, who died suddenly at thirty-one. She was devastated. My grandmother lost both her son and her husband within two years of one another.

Perhaps it was her grief, perhaps she needed to put some distance between those losses and herself, but soon enough, Mam decided to leave New Jersey for Arizona. Our entire family otherwise remained in New Jersey, unable to afford to visit her.

I became numb. I didn't deal with my uncle's loss, and I couldn't comprehend my life without Mam nearby. I began to disengage emotionally, especially from my relationship. I didn't know how to talk about my life to other people. I was afraid of being judged.

People at work thought I was single, and I was getting a lot of attention. I liked it because I felt so disconnected. Outside of work, in my gay circle, some of the women were flirting with me, and I liked that too. It never occurred to me that my flirtations might cause my partner to feel insecure. She would randomly say, "I don't know if this is what I really want," and become emotionally distant. I didn't know how to handle that, and it was me who ultimately became insecure.

I started seeking validation and approval outside of myself and outside of our relationship, even though my partner and I were moving toward a long-term commitment by buying a house. It was a big decision, and I grappled with my indiscretions. I was filled with remorse and felt unworthy. I loved her and what we had together, but could I be faithful? Honest? Did I trust that she would endure hardships and successes with me? And could she trust the same in me?

Filled with insecurity about her discontentment, I questioned her ability to commit.

We made the decision to buy the house, but she seemed gripped by fear shortly after we moved in. My partner became emotionally paralyzed. She started going out with a 'friend' who was an ex of one of our other friends. I never trusted this person because when she'd dated our friend, she would often say to me that she wanted what I had. Because of this, I started to grow suspicious as my partner completely disengaged from participating in activities that were needed to make the house one's own. She became emotionally unavailable and superficial.

After a few months, I became angry. I'd had enough. I packed up all her things one night when she was out with her 'friend' and put them in the garage.

I called my aunt and told her what I'd done. She understood my feelings and agreed that something needed to happen, but she wanted me to think through my actions regardless. She said that all relationships go through hard times, but those relationships that work through hard times strengthen and last. While those that didn't, wouldn't.

Ours didn't, and I ended up grieving many losses at once.

Our house was bought with two salaries. I had no idea how I was going to manage since I didn't earn enough to cover the costs. Mam was moving and wanted me to assume responsibility for my mother and my siblings. I was overwhelmed by the obligation and chaos. Managing my mother was a full-time job, and we struggled to communicate. I couldn't have open and honest adult conversations with her. And problem solving together was non-existent because she would take things personally, yell, and criticize me for being selfish, then abruptly end conversations by hanging up or leaving the room, which created bitterness in me. And my sister, very much like my mother, had two children she couldn't parent. Meanwhile, my brother was devastated over the loss of our uncle, and he was collapsing too.

The expectation of my role in my family as the oldest child was that I would handle it. And although I said I could, I started to fall apart. And to make matters worse, while I'd always relied on my aunt and uncle to guide me, we had a significant misunderstanding that resulted in a serious falling out. I was an emotional mess. The two people whom I'd loved, trusted, and counted on as much as I did my grandmother had thrown me out of their lives.

Words couldn't describe the feelings of betrayal. I couldn't make sense of what had happened. My relationship with my aunt and uncle had been special. I'd felt loved and a sense of stability and belonging. I had no idea what I'd done to create such antipathy, resulting in complete abandonment. *It's over*, I thought. *I no longer belonged.*

Everything was unraveling. And I was alone.

Hollow, I threw myself into work. It seemed to be my only escape. I trudged through life, becoming short-tempered, impatient, dismissive, and more arrogant, especially if I felt unheard or misunderstood.

I returned to the resourcefulness that had worked for me in college. I started cleaning houses after my day job to supplement my income. I couldn't bear changing jobs. I rented a room out in my house and shopped at estate and yard sales to slowly furnish it. I brought lunch to physicians at least once a week and acted as if I was cleaning up the leftovers, but I took them home and sometimes even shared them with the homeless people I encountered in the inner city.

My drinking started to increase as I lamented the sorry state of my life. My ex and I were friends before we had a relationship, and we maintained a healthy friendship following it. She called me weekly, and at one point, she said, "You seem hung over a lot. What's going on?" *What's going on?* I said to myself. *Life sucks! It's not fair!* I was disillusioned and angry. I pretended all was okay externally and that I was happy and having fun. I acted positive, but inside, my soul had turned bitter, and I slowly went deeper into my isolation.

Despairing about being alone and having to manage my life's responsibilities was daunting. I sought help and went to therapy again.

My fear of being alone intensified my quest to find someone; I was nearing thirty and was filled with doubt that I would ever find a life partner.

Dating was difficult, and I realized it was unlikely I'd meet someone who wanted a committed relationship in a bar. Instead, I networked with friends and went to different events. I met some nice people, but I didn't realize how needy I was.

Since I was insecure, I tended to dive in quickly and was too serious. Most people wanted to ease in, but I was intense. I started the dating game and found that, in some cases, people had more baggage than me, and I quickly moved on. While in other situations, I was obviously the one with the baggage and the other person quickly moved on instead. I started to doubt myself and my ability to pick a potential mate that was good for me. I questioned whether I had the capacity to truly love another person, given my experiences with my mother and my new responsibility for her.

Somewhere along the journey, someone told me that we attract on the outside what we project from the inside. I failed to heed that lesson. Rather than work on my self-esteem and insecurity, I focused on my appearance, believing I was unattractive.

I have an uncanny ability to find humor in most things, but when it came to finding a life partner, I couldn't. I started to despair. I felt like I was seeking but never finding and then finding but not keeping. Something clearly was wrong with me, and I couldn't understand what.

Most of my friends were heterosexual. They were getting married and having children. But even my gay friends were settling down. I started to believe I would be alone for the rest of my life. My friends tried to help keep me grounded by reminding me of the successful relationship I'd had before and encouraging me to be patient. "The right person would appear." "It would all work out in time." *Yeah right, when?* I was filled with uncertainty.

My therapist focused first on my fear and insecurity. He suggested two books, *The Two Step: The Dance Toward Intimacy* by Eileen McCann and *Getting the Love That You Want* by Harville Hendrix. We talked a lot about recognizing fear while dating and changing behavior in the face of it.

I worked hard in therapy, and over time, I identified what I needed and wanted from a life partner. I had lots of things to practice when I finally found someone to date. I came to terms with what had worked and what hadn't in my last relationship. In the process, I realized that I still loved and adored my ex, even if in a different way than before.

We were very similar on many levels, but we had different wants and needs. We agreed we were friends first, above all else, and understood each other, nourished and encouraged each other to overcome whatever we faced in life. We vowed to stay in one another's lives and support each other throughout the journey.

Though sadly, as in any relationship, gay or straight, exes staying in each other's lives often creates suspicion or jealously with a new life partner. We didn't think about that until we were faced with that reality. And, ultimately, we were forced to move on from one another completely.

I will always love her and cherish the life experiences we shared together.

I didn't want to admit that I believed I was not good enough for anyone and that I was afraid of being alone. I was a lone wolf, after all. I was a survivor, self-reliant, and successful in my own right. But the truth was, I was protecting myself.

I needed my family, as dysfunctional as they were.

My therapist suggested I create new traditions apart from my aunt and uncle.

I live my life with music to help me manage change. No matter what is going on, happy or sad, I find a song to get me through it. To manage the loss of my relationship with my aunt and uncle and their family, I sang lyrics from a song I knew from childhood written by Joni Mitchell, "Both Sides Now." The words "something's lost, but something's gained in living every day" describe how I managed through that change.

I followed the guidance of my therapist and reunited my mother, Lisa and her two children, and my brother Bo. We all needed each other, and we had our first Christmas together as a family, just us. My mother was thrilled, and I realized this could be our new tradition.

Although my mom and I both mourned the loss of the big family gatherings we both loved and cherished during the holidays with Mam and Pop, we began anew. Each year, my mom, Lisa and the kids, and my brother would attend my annual party the Sunday before Christmas, then we enjoyed Christmas Eve together. While I greatly missed celebrating with my aunts and uncles, being with my immediate family brought me peace and some joy. I felt like we were the island of misfit toys; none of us belonged. But in those moments, we had a sense of belonging.

When I was finally willing to be vulnerable with my mom and siblings, I made some progress. I started to become more comfortable. Prior to that, I didn't know what to do with myself when I was alone, but my therapist provided me with tools and suggestions I had to use. I had to open my mind and try, and when I did, things started to change on the inside, and being alone wasn't as scary.

My therapist used to say, "The minute you become comfortable being alone, you'll see. You'll meet the love of your life." A wise man.

Aunt Ann always said your twenties are called the 'turbulent twenties' for a reason. I realize now that as I neared the end of my twenties, the turbulence had all been about relationship fear: living my truth, being accepted at work, building a network of friends, accepting my role in the family, and finding and keeping the love of my life.

The challenge, though, was that my mind was filled with negative beliefs triggered by fear, and those beliefs followed me as I moved along into the next stage of my journey.

Lost in the Tumultuous Sea

Well-being. Feeling comfortable, healthy, and happy was my pursuit as I entered my thirties.

I continued working with my therapist, and I practiced feeling fear and doing things anyway. I cooked for myself. I ate meals alone. I found solace working with my hands inside and outside of the house. I refurbished my old home to its original splendor. I created a garden and brought back the beauty of the original landscaping, and I was happy at work again. Life was good. There wasn't a cloud in the sky, and I didn't anticipate any possible storms in the forecast.

I met the love of my life six months after turning thirty, and I knew at the end of our first date that I wanted to spend the rest of my life with her. She was the one. Yet, for once, I didn't jump in. I managed my fear.

Eileen McCann's book, *The Two Step*, helped me understand the underlying fear that each person may feel in the dance toward intimacy, and I spent therapy sessions processing my fear and how to use the tools when faced with it. It worked.

We took our time getting to know each other, and when I was gripped with insecurity and feeling restless, I redirected. I called my friends. I worked in the yard. I went for walks. I grappled with my crazy, fear-based thoughts that I wasn't pretty enough, or she wouldn't like me if she knew about my family, or that I wasn't good enough for her.

Like most new relationships, ours was very exciting in the beginning. We spent time together doing things we enjoyed, and I felt content even when we sat quietly in silence. She was the only person who understood and acknowledged my feelings of aloneness with my family. She said, "So you take care of everyone, but no one takes care of you? That must be hard." "Yes," I said, while tears of sadness combined with tears of joy streamed down my face. I was understood by a potential life partner! She was so beautiful, so kind, so special. She opened my heart again, and I felt safe with her.

Until I didn't.

She had her own life experiences and desires. Her pursuit of well-being included a one-year cycling trip across western Europe and other parts of the world. She was a planner and planned a sabbatical from her job. I was impressed, but I was also gripped by fear. My mind was beset with all sorts of questions and what-if scenarios. Would she meet someone better than me, someone who was just as athletic as she was? Would she end up living in Europe? What would I do if something bad happened to her?

I managed through my fears and did my best to come to terms with the inevitable truth that she was going to travel for a year, whether I liked it or not. I had to trust that it would work out. I had to trust her.

Our relationship progressed, and months before she left, we decided to be exclusive. We agreed that we were in a committed relationship. Then, the night came: She told me it was best that we end things. I did not see that coming at all. Just days before, we were talking about how I could visit her while she was on her trip. I was completely stunned.

I handled the breakup calmly. I didn't cry and beg her to stay or criticize and blame—common behavior in the face of fear. Rather, I recognized that she probably had her own fears too. I quietly told her that I was sad about her decision, but I also asked her to leave. I handled it with courage until she left. Only once she had stepped out of the house did I freak out, and the old negative thinking returned.

She called and left a message, wanting to get together and talk about it, but I was the hurt lone wolf, afraid to trust and be vulnerable. The negative thoughts were screaming in my head, "You can't trust anyone! She doesn't really care! She just feels sorry for you!"

I didn't return her calls. What was she going to say? "It's not you, it's me." I was sick of that line. "I love you like a friend and want you in my life." No, that's not happening. I had enough friends.

There was no need to talk. I knew how it was going to go, and I wasn't having it.

But she was persistent.

She called a mutual friend, someone who understood my life story and the work I was doing in therapy. Our friend knew how I felt before the breakup, and she challenged me to overcome my fear and negative thinking. "So, you're going to let your fear hold you back and miss out on the opportunity of a lifetime?" she asked. "You know this is what you want. What are you going to gain by protecting yourself?"

I responded, "She obviously wasn't genuine, because if she really cared about me, she wouldn't have done this."

She scoffed, "Geez, if she wasn't genuine and didn't care about you, do you really think she would have gone out of her way to call me? Think about that."

Those words hit me hard.

I did want to get back together. I wanted to spend the rest of my life with her. But all I thought was, *If only she hadn't done that, then I would be able to trust and get back together with her.* I was protecting myself and retreating to the place that was safest—alone and unhappy. Through reflection, I realized that the barrier wasn't what had happened—it was my fear of never getting the love that I wanted. Trust required me to be willing to take a risk despite uncertainty. I wasn't protecting myself; I was afraid, and my thinking was holding me back. It was only a matter of *being willing* to be vulnerable. That was all it would take to overcome my fear and take a step forward.

Was she worth the risk? Absolutely. So, I took the risk.

We met up, and she was vulnerable with me. She expressed her own fears and how she thought breaking up might be safer for her. She obviously thought through how she'd been protecting herself, and she was willing to take a risk with me too.

That was the best decision of my life.

Before she left for her trip, life was magical. We spent time with and enjoyed her family, and we traveled and found our happy place: the dunes of Provincetown, Massachusetts. We had a profound experience in Maui, Hawaii, on a trip that I won at work. I loved her, and I loved life. I felt safe and secure at last. No storm could blow my world apart again, surely.

But in a matter of weeks after returning from Hawaii, Mam died, my company was acquired, my partner left for her trip, and a dear friend passed away from AIDS. Once more, my world had turned upside down.

Losing my grandmother hurt. I took for granted that she would live a long life. I visited her with a colleague the first year she moved to Arizona en route to a national sales meeting, and then again during a vacation with a woman I'd been dating. In both instances, I didn't visit with Mam for very long, nor did I spend quality time with her.

After she died, I realized that I never appreciated how lonely she must have been without our family. During each visit, she was eager to show me things in her home, tell me about what was happening in her life, and take me to see things she thought were beautiful or out to a show. These were all things we enjoyed together. But I was always with friends, and I mistakenly believed there would always be another trip for all of that.

One of our last conversations before she died was about the importance of doing things while you're young. Mam loved to travel because she enjoyed experiencing different cultures and seeing life's beauty. She endured a very hard life with my grandfather, lost everything, rebuilt it, saved and saved, and waited until her retirement to see the things she'd always dreamed about. Sadly, her body had changed as she aged. She had physical limitations and couldn't do most of the things she'd hoped to do.

She encouraged me to travel and see each of the fifty states and, most importantly, to see the world. She said that no matter what my financial situation was, to do what it would take. "Don't let finances hold you back." She lived to share experiences with those she loved and encouraged me to do the same.

I have some regrets in my life, and the greatest is not spending quality time with Mam during the last three years of her life. I failed to give back.

Losing my grandmother was one of my biggest and most profound losses. She'd been my guardian angel, my role model, my inspiration, my mother, my disciplinarian, and my rock. Without her, Aunt Ann, and Uncle Tim, I felt alone despite the contentment in my relationship.

My aunt Ann knew how much Mam meant to me, and she invited me to join the rest of our family at her house. But given the falling out we'd had and the sense of betrayal I'd felt, I was afraid to be vulnerable around my family again, especially in the throes of grief. I needed boundaries, even though, deep down, I wanted to be with them freely. Regardless, I spoke honestly with my aunt, and she understood. I made a healthy choice for myself, but it was hard.

My partner hadn't yet met my family, but she supported my decision. She comforted me greatly. We planted flowers in my garden to help me process my grief.

Following the funeral service, I joined my family for a meal at my Uncle Tim's house. My aunt and others were eager to make amends from years earlier, but I was numb and lost. Negative thinking prevailed. As much as I yearned for closeness, I believed what was best was to love from a distance. I accepted their apologies but expressed that I didn't have a desire to regain what we once had. I felt safer.

We spent time with my partner's family often. They were small and close-knit. They had many friends and extended family and had nice traditions and fun gatherings. I loved spending time with them. I loved her mother and stepfather. We had intellectually stimulating discussions and, most importantly, great laughs.

We had many family dinners, spent holidays together, and went on family trips. We enjoyed one another and created great memories. We grew very close. I felt loved and accepted by them. Deep down, however, I still felt incomplete. I missed dancing and laughing with my own family. I felt like a part of my life was gone. The old feelings of not belonging crept back in from time to time, and I didn't know how to deal with them. But rather than take the risk and engage with my aunt and uncle, I pushed my feelings down. I wasn't willing to admit that I needed them back in my life. I continued to choose distance.

Navigating family landed me on a desert island. Navigating my career, however, had me swimming in a tumultuous, stormy sea.

Shortly after returning from the incentive trip to Maui, my company announced that it had been acquired. My manager met with me right away and indicated there may no longer be a role for me. The acquiring company had an employee assigned to the area I worked in, and there was little chance they would assign two people. My manager encouraged me to leave on my own accord since I was at the top of my game, believing there would be more opportunity for me on a number of levels. And having worked with him for over six years, I trusted him. Despite the uncertainty and being afraid of change, I heeded his guidance.

I was hired by one of the fastest-growing and top-performing companies in the pharmaceutical industry. A friend worked there, and another had recently been hired. I felt comfortable knowing a few people since the company was so big, but the transition was difficult. Although there'd been limited growth opportunities at my previous company, I'd been given extra duties and special assignments. I thrived there. I'd been like a big fish in a small pond. But with the new company, I was a guppy in the ocean.

Old feelings of insecurity at work came back and showed up as arrogance. I thought that, given my years in the industry, I might be eligible for accelerated advancement. After accepting the position, I learned that wasn't the case. I'd been too caught up with the best company wanting to hire me rather than ensuring I was making a good career choice. I dreaded having to start over and prove myself again, so I jumped in blind.

The job began with one month away from home for training, but unlike my first company, this was an intense immersive training.

Knowledge tests were given daily, and when a person scored below 90, they were fired. The pressure was immense. Nobody slept. I watched people new to the industry get sick and break down from the pressure.

The leadership in the company prided themselves on what they called a culture of excellence. I wasn't used to that. I wondered if all large companies operated like that, since I didn't have a framework from which to measure. My experience in the small company was a culture that was supportive and collaborative, but this was a dog-eat-dog environment that thrived on survival.

Despite feeling miserable, I successfully completed what felt like boot camp. On some level, I was proud of my achievement, since several people didn't make it. I was happy to move on and get started with my job, confident in my abilities. But I was also exhausted and needed time to recover.

My manager had other plans. He'd picked up on my arrogance and chided me often, saying I had to get everything I thought I knew about the industry out of my head. He wanted me to unlearn everything I'd internalized while at my previous company. He said he was going to break me. I couldn't understand the rationale and struggled with the tactics he used.

His expectations were beyond high. He wanted me to report to work in the South Bronx, New York, by 7 a.m. and entertain customers daily over lunch and dinner. If I didn't have a customer dinner, he expected me to work until 6 p.m. He even had someone come to my home to organize the drawers in my filing cabinet in my home office, and he called me at home at 5 a.m. every day.

I'd endured six weeks with no sleep, and I still wasn't sleeping. The area I was assigned was crime-ridden and one hour from home without traffic. Customers thought I was crazy for working there. There were shootings daily, and they told me scary stories about bad things that happened to pharmaceutical representatives. I became hypervigilant while driving and walking from my car to the customer's office. Buildings were abandoned and burned out and, one day, I saw a young boy playing in collapsed building rubble using a sink pipe and bottles to practice hitting a ball. I cried.

The pressure from my manager combined with the intense fear affected me. I rarely saw my partner before she left for her trip, and when I did, I was irritable, argumentative, or negative about my job and family.

Lisa continued to struggle with raising her two kids. She needed a job but didn't have a car. Her bipolar disorder was not yet diagnosed, and I thought that if I bought her a car, it might help. I also tried to visit weekly to check on her and the kids. She didn't live in a safe area, and I grew concerned when my toddler niece showed me the loaded gun she'd found. I had no idea what my sister was involved in, but it wasn't good.

Buying the car enabled Lisa to work. Unfortunately, having money enabled her to buy drugs. She was an addict, although I didn't realize it at the time.

At one point, she admitted to me that she was hooked on drugs and needed help. She even asked me to take her children and care for them, but I didn't trust her and, given the pressure at work, I said no. Instead, I continued to visit, and from the outside, everything looked okay. Or so it seemed.

My mental health declined even more. I was emotional, quick to anger, suspicious, and distrustful. Everyone in my life was concerned. My partner was cycling through Europe, and we talked twice a week, and each time, she encouraged me to quit. "This job isn't worth it. You're so talented, you can get another one." She wanted the happy and content me back. The problem was, I couldn't see that I'd even left.

I'd never failed at anything before, and I believed that quitting my job meant I was a failure. I missed Mam and Aunt Ann, and I believed I needed their help to think things through. I didn't have time for therapy anymore, and although I tried to talk to my mom about things instead, and she tried to the best of her capabilities, I couldn't connect with her on the level I needed. I was on the verge of a nervous breakdown.

During the long drives at 6 a.m. each day, I started to think life wasn't worth living anymore.

And although I didn't have the courage to kill myself, I started fantasizing about getting drunk and dying in a car accident.

Despite it all, there was light in my storm. I visited my partner in Italy, and shortly afterward, she made the decision to cut her trip short and return home. We moved in together.

I was about six months into the job when my manager directed me to do something unethical within our industry. I realized then that he must have thought he'd broken me. And I was broken, but not completely.

I resigned, but I didn't deal with the effect the job had on my mental health, nor did I take a breather. Rather, I quickly secured another position with a competing company and started over. I started to have difficulty with others wherever I turned. I inevitably would say something that offended someone, and I couldn't understand why.

At my first company, I'd been open with my manager about my background, so whenever I did or said something that was inappropriate or unprofessional, he addressed me right away and helped me understand what I did wrong and how to handle it differently. I appreciated his open communication style and learned and grew professionally.

Thankfully, overall, the culture at the company I moved to following the unethical incident at the last was very similar to the first company I'd worked for. It was supportive and collaborative, and I quickly excelled. I was fast-tracked for promotion. I received praise and recognition from my manager and other members of the leadership team—but the attention started to go to my head again.

During an off-site meeting, I observed during a team building softball game that my manager, who was in the infield, seemed to chase the ball no matter where on the field the ball was. He and I often had many philosophical conversations about leadership, and I was struck that he thought he had to play every position on the team. When I shared my observation with him afterwards, he became enraged. He was Hindu and, as an American woman, I was completely unmindful of our cultural differences. Although I thought I was being sincere when I started the conversation, from his reaction, I realized he misunderstood my intention and felt criticized. There was no way for me to break through his anger. He called our team together and told them what I'd said, and then—one by one—asked if they thought what I said was true. My teammates were dumbfounded and looked at me with dismay.

They distanced themselves from me, and I understood why.

At the time, I was being considered for a promotion, but my manager no longer supported it. He actively worked to block it, though he was unsuccessful. I received the promotion anyway, but I was met with many obstacles afterward.

The position required that I work jointly with members of my previous team. Despite that, my former manager forbade them from working with me. Regardless, I managed to be successful and won another performance award, which included another incentive trip. I was fast-tracked for a second promotion to the training department at corporate headquarters. It was a position I wanted.

I was on the incentive trip when the regional director invited me to join her for dinner. I was thrilled and honored; the promotion to the training department was conditional upon her support. During dinner, however, a colleague brought up a topic, and I didn't agree with her position on it, so I shared my thoughts freely.

My colleague had to interrupt. "So, you think your role is more important than mine?" I said no and went on to explain what I meant, but I was abruptly interrupted again, this time by the regional director, who emphatically said, "Yes, you do think you're more important!" She said that I would never amount to anything in my career.

I tried to meet separately with her later to understand what I did or said wrong, but she refused. I felt dejected. I didn't know what to do. I got drunk and wept with anyone who'd listen.

When I returned from the incentive trip, my manager told me I was selected for the position in the training department, but that I no longer had the support of the regional director for the promotion. I was devastated, but my manager told me not to give up. He educated me on the politics of a big company and shared with me various approaches to deal with a situation like the one that I was in. He had a plan.

Unfortunately, I didn't learn a thing. I couldn't hear his teachings, nor his plan. I was in my head, having a pity party. *I'm never going to succeed*, played over and over in my mind.

I started yelling at truck drivers while on the road to work, telling strangers off, and drinking. I was so angry with myself and the world. I ranted in my head that people only cared about themselves. That they all lied and couldn't be trusted, so why bother? I convinced myself that even if my manager succeeded in getting me the promotion, I wasn't going to accept it. The thought of navigating the corporate environment scared me. *Besides,* I said to myself, *why stay? Nobody cares about my professional growth and development, anyway.*

That wasn't true. My manager cared. He was supportive, and he wanted to see me succeed. He was working hard to help me overcome the obstacles I'd created in my path, but I couldn't see his efforts, nor could I appreciate his support. I was looking at life through a straw. I only focused on what I didn't have—the support of the regional director—rather than what I did have—the support of my manager and many others in the company who wanted me on their team.

I was afraid of never getting what I wanted in my career, and this fear held me back.

Instead, I pursued an unexpected opportunity with a medical communications company I learned about from a colleague at the previous company. I had no idea what medical communications was, but I was so blinded by self-pity, I accepted the position immediately. My motive was purely to prove to the regional director that I would go somewhere in my career. I believed I would have the opportunity to build relationships with marketing executives, and that if I proved myself, I would be back in a marketing position within two years.

When I resigned, however, my manager was disappointed. He'd been able to secure support to promote me to another area of training. The hiring manager called me and reviewed the opportunity and stressed how the role would set me up for future career growth within the company. But I merely thanked him and maintained my decision to leave.

Unexpectedly, when my resignation was communicated throughout the company, I received an outpouring of phone calls from colleagues encouraging me to stay. I was overwhelmed. Where had that come from? People actually liked me and cared? I wasn't able to see through the fog of my internal storm.

The transition to medical communications felt eerily similar to my transition to pharmaceutical sales. I went from knowing what to do to be successful to an abyss of unknowns. In pharmaceutical sales, I sold a product with messaging developed for me; I was a messenger. In medical communications, however, I was selling ideas and the successful implementation of them. I didn't know how to lead that, and there wasn't any training. It was trial by fire. The role challenged me to go beyond my experience and pull my creative and problem-solving skills from the depths of my being.

I was assigned to the company I had resigned from, and I was filled with self-doubt. I worried about what my former colleagues would think because I didn't know what I was doing. I was afraid of looking incompetent in front of my peers. What the hell was I thinking? What on earth had I gotten myself into? Those questions ran through my mind, over and over. But I'd been in this situation before, and despite my fear, I was determined. And it helped that the work seemed stimulating, and I loved problem solving.

During my first year, I endured failure after failure, but I learned from each one. I persevered. I met with various clients and gained insight and feedback on what made a good medical communications partner. I met with members of the internal team to understand their roles and my role and the relationship between the two. People said they liked my approach, and the more I learned, the more refined my approach to sales became.

I sold a small project to a client who was willing to take a chance with our company. We performed well, and the client referred us to the senior director of marketing for the brand.

I met with the senior director, and she also complimented us on our work. She offered us an opportunity, but in order to proceed, she wanted a commitment from me. "When I make a buying decision, I buy the person who sold me, because I believe they know what I need and want. I don't want to be handed off to someone else who doesn't know my strategy and plan. It's bullshit, and it's frustrating!" If we were to work with her, we had to commit that I would lead the successful implementation of the project. I had no idea what that meant, but I spoke to my manager about it.

My manager was one of the owners, and he said we would give her whatever she wanted. I would be the lead and the point of contact, and, in turn, the client awarded us a sizeable contract, one that doubled the sales of the company.

That had been the easy part. The implementation took a coordinated, multidisciplinary, cross-functional team that had operational processes, attention to detail, outstanding communication, and trainers for new team members. Our company didn't have any of that.

The first dilemma was not having any internal resources available for the project. I spoke to the vice president of operations and was told I had to hire and build my own team. What the hell? Build my own team? I had zero experience. I had no sense of how to evaluate and hire talent. I had no idea what I needed. There was no training and no one to guide me. Panic settled in.

My first inclination was to call the client and tell her we couldn't deliver. But I spoke to my manager instead, and he assured me they would hire, build, and train the logistics team. All I had to do was find a medical writer and a graphic designer.

That was the start of a very chaotic, yet exhilarating journey.

I worked with our art director to find a graphic designer. When I told the graphic designer about my plight, she introduced me to a medical writer. And the three of us complemented each other. We collaborated, figured things out, and produced quality work. We became a unit. I loved working with them.

My challenge was with the poorly organized operational infrastructure in the company. I felt uneasy.

The client and I had weekly meetings. We discussed the implementation process, and she mapped out every step of each component of the project. I learned so much from her. She had an amazing presence and was an incredible leader and mentor. I wanted to be like her someday. I was so unsure of myself, and I didn't want to disappoint her. I found myself calling her incessantly for guidance, to the point of frustrating her. "I hired you because I thought you could lead this shit! If you're insecure, we've got to talk, because I don't have time to manage everything on my plate and manage you too!"

Rather than collapsing in insecurity, I realized that it didn't matter what processes or resources or training we had or didn't have. I had to take an active role in figuring it out. That is what leadership is all about. If it meant developing processes, I had to be involved in developing them. If it meant getting my hands dirty, I had to get involved. Self-reliance had propelled me out of poverty. I had to find my confidence and rely on my ability to lead.

I led the team, and although we had bumps along the way, we had a successful outcome. But my work became all-consuming.

Finding time to visit my niece and nephew became more and more difficult. I visited when I could. And I started to notice that they didn't have the things I was buying them. Things like clothes, shoes, and a winter coat were missing. They started to appear unkempt, and Lisa seemed to be moving to different apartments frequently. I was too busy at work to get involved and try to figure out what was going on, but I asked my mother if she suspected anything, and she said no. She saw Lisa and the kids almost weekly.

Eventually, I received a call from the Division of Youth and Family Services. They'd received an anonymous call and were investigating it. They were concerned for the children and wanted to see if either my mother or I would be able to take them, otherwise they were going to be placed in foster care.

I went to Lisa's apartment and discovered she no longer lived there. I tracked her down in a drug den—with her kids.

My niece and nephew were living a very similar life to what I'd experienced when I lived with my mother and stepfather, but the ravages of addiction that my niece and nephew endured were far greater. It was too much for me to bear. Only then did I recall that years before, Lisa told me that she was a drug addict and needed help, but I hadn't believed her. I was filled with guilt and remorse. I was so angry at Lisa and even angrier at myself.

I pursued joint custody with my mother. One of the saddest days of my life was testifying against my drug-addicted sister. She was so high on heroin that she had no idea that we were taking her kids away. We were distraught.

My mom wanted the kids to live with her, and I reluctantly agreed, but the strain on me was still immense. My mom lived in a small one-bedroom apartment, and she relied on public transportation or coworkers to get back and forth to work. I had to figure out many things quickly.

I bought a condo to accommodate my mom and the kids and hired a woman who could help me take care of them. I wanted to believe that my mother could do it, but with her history, I didn't trust that she could.

While this was going on with my family, the client awarded us an even bigger contract and another client we'd pitched awarded us a large project as well. Those wins caused the company to grow rapidly, which was both a blessing and a curse. We had to expand the team; we needed new processes and had no one to develop them. We needed training on the new processes and we only had one manager to lead and supervise all employees. And we had to build a new team comprising different roles and skill sets to develop training workshops that would be rolled out across the United States. It was a recipe for gross error and implementation failure.

Shortly after launching the projects, we were beset with issues from every direction.

Self-reliance is a trait regarded as positive or negative. It's positive when seen in a child, teen, or young adult because it refers to independence and autonomy. But it's perceived as negative in an adult because it refers to reliance on one's own powers and resources rather than leaning on the support of others.

When faced with the pressure of handling a significant operational failure, I resorted to self-reliance. It's what I knew. I designed processes, trained the staff myself, and made myself available to the extended clients for calls so I could troubleshoot. I single-handedly addressed every problem. But was I a hero?

No.

Self-reliance was my go-to as a child, and in the face of fear of losing the business, it was my only solution. I believed I couldn't rely on anyone, and in the process of taking charge, I lost myself.

I worked day and night; clients yelled all day, every day. My manager was uninvolved. He didn't seem to care about what was happening. I yelled at everyone. I was overwhelming already overwhelmed people. We didn't have support, and the operations leader didn't know what to do.

Self-reliance no longer worked, and I had no other tool in my toolbox.

And at the same time, I was dealing with my mentally ill mother and trying to co-parent with her. The kids were neglected and had many needs: clothes, health checkups, dentist appointments, behavioral and learning disability evaluation and management. I was attending school meetings and doctor visits while getting called incessantly to tackle problems at work.

I began to think I was being punished by God. I thought life was unfair. I was lonely, despite objectively having my partner's support. I was never home, and I missed her. I missed my aunt and uncle. I missed spending time with family and our friends. I missed laughing. I was tired, and I was bitter.

Nobody cared. I couldn't rely on anyone. Nobody was genuine. I needed help. I couldn't deal with the pressure, and I started drinking heavily to relieve it.

What had happened to me? Where was the happy-go-lucky Tracy who laughed and had fun? I was lost in the tumultuous sea and could no longer navigate my ship through the storm.

The fantasy of getting drunk and dying in a car accident returned. But this time, the fantasy became a reality.

Yet, I lived.

Eye of the Storm
The Reaction Cascade

I don't know how I lived.

I was a hair away from a head-on collision with an SUV when my car came to a complete stop. Faced with the reality of my death wish, I'd realized that I'd been given a choice.

It's A Wonderful Life, an oldie but a goodie, was and remains my favorite holiday movie. The main character, George Bailey, sacrifices himself for his family and foregoes what he wants for himself. By his mid-thirties, when faced with his family business going bankrupt, he believes his only solution is jumping off a bridge, sure that he and everyone around him would be better off if he were dead. But George's guardian angel appears and shows him what the world would be like without him—spoiler alert, after seeing how the lives of the people he loved and cared for turned out without him, he cries out to God on the bridge, "I want to live again!"

I emotionally identified with George Bailey. By my mid-thirties, I was embittered and nihilistic. My destiny seemed to be one of sacrifices for my family and for my job. I felt like I didn't have a choice. My bitterness and anger simmered just beneath the surface. To some, it was evident. To others, I was successful and fun-loving and a woman who went above and beyond and took care of or helped others. But in reality, I was slowly rotting on the inside. My mantra had become, "Life sucks, and then you die."

Where had I gone? What happened to me? How did I get so lost?

I was emotionally burned out. Completely bankrupt.

A black stone existed in my soul that fed on hate and bitterness, and I didn't know how to free myself from it. I was living with an internal, tumultuous storm I couldn't navigate my way out of, and as I held tighter to the bitterness and anger, my emotional well-being was affected, as well as the well-being of those around me. I struggled daily in my relationships.

On the one hand, I went above and beyond to please people, but I felt like it was never good enough. On the other hand, I seemed to think that I knew it all and didn't need any help with anything. Yet when I felt unheard, I yelled to be heard; when I felt misunderstood, I would fight to be right; and when I felt unappreciated, I became angry and critical. At times, I did or said inappropriate things or reacted with an intensity that wasn't commensurate with the situation. My words and actions pushed people away, and I didn't know how to change it.

Like the character George Bailey, I wanted to live again, but I didn't know how to. I felt like I was a human doing, not a human being. I felt disconnected and just wanted to learn how to be and to find peace within.

Having studied psychology, I knew deep down that the death wish fantasies were suicidal thoughts. I needed medication, but

I didn't want to accept that I needed that type of help. I thought I could somehow work my way through it, despite evidence that this wasn't possible. But I was eventually prescribed an antidepressant, which I took daily.

I'd been in and out of therapy for years and was upset because I couldn't seem to function without it. Lucky for me, my therapist was a firm believer that you work on what you set out to overcome and then move on. I'd done that with my intimacy issues, and we agreed it was time to work on my anger.

After a year, I was feeling better. My doctor took me off the antidepressant, and with new tools from therapy in my toolbox, I finally set sail.

Within six or seven months, however, I found myself struggling to be understood again.

I'd started a new job as a senior vice president with a start-up company on the cutting edge of our line of business. Since I'd worn each hat for the delivery of services in my previous position, I had very fixed ideas on how operations should run. But my subordinates didn't agree.

I struggled with open-mindedness. When team members brought different approaches to the table, my narrow-mindedness shut others' ideas down, and my dismissiveness caused angst and frustration. When people didn't do what I asked, or if I felt misunderstood, I became arrogant, frustrated, or angry.

Despite medical intervention and trying to use the tools learned in therapy, I was back to that place where I didn't know how to be. I was lost and stuck in the storm, as I always seemed to end up every time I was 'done' with therapy.

I went back to some of the self-help books I loved in my early career as a counselor. From the *Four Agreements* by Don Miguel Ruiz, I reflected on the concepts he discussed about the belief system, the Book of Law, and fear. I concluded that I was judgmental and had a victim mentality that was tied to old wounds and beliefs. Fear seemed to be the driver of my reactions, and therefore, the cause of my difficulties. According to Ruiz, fear manifests in anger, jealousy, hate, envy, and other negative emotions, and I was intrigued by the idea of 'mitote'—a Toltec word—that means nobody understands each other because we're not able to see ourselves and how we really are.

We're all blinded by our old beliefs that are shaped by our life experiences. Those old ideas combine with fear and limit us from seeing the truth about ourselves. This "fog" prevents us from changing and becoming the person we want to be.

The Four Agreements are powerful and require daily practice. But of course, I didn't stick with them for long. I wanted a quick fix, and so I kept struggling. I have since learned that changing our mindset is a process that takes time and that changing our mindset for the long-term requires daily practice to maintain.

Regardless, the Four Agreements inspired me to embark on a new journey of self-discovery and healing: How could I deal with fear?

I went back to another book that helped me during the turbulent twenties, *Feel the Fear... and Do It Anyway* by Susan Jeffers. I was wounded, and my life experiences had caused me to develop a victim mentality that I was obviously acting on. It was time to revisit and tackle those fears since they caused anger and negative emotions. I already had tools for anger, which meant I needed tools for fear if I truly wanted to change.

Through that book, I rediscovered that we all live with some kind of fear, but victim thinking limits us, and change happens when we retrain our thinking and find the power within ourselves.

I applied some of the strategies she reviewed, like feeling the fear and doing things anyway, listening to my never-ending negative and critical thoughts (or "chatterbox," as she called it), and using the affirmations she suggested to redirect them.

I went on to read many more books which all advanced the idea of retraining the mind to find personal power and transform, yet I found myself having difficulty making the connection to my belief system. Each time I would have a reaction, I would ask why. Why does this keep happening? I justified and explained why: It was because of my mother or stepfather; it was because of this; it was because of that ...

Jeffers specifically challenges us to take responsibility for our life and our reactions, but I remained in this victim place I couldn't understand how to get out of. She talked about how we're afraid to change, and therefore, resist it. Jeffers encourages risk-taking, meaning talking about our fear with others who are also working on themselves and building a support system.

I had to come to terms with my resistance.

Being vulnerable to me meant being weak. But to commit to changing from being the one-way mirror to being vulnerable, I had to trust people. That was hard for me, though I inevitably made a conscious decision to trust one specific friend, and that's how my journey began. It ultimately expanded to include other friends, colleagues, family, and in some instances, even strangers I met on a plane—but it started by trusting just *one* person, by giving myself permission to let one person in just a little.

As I talked openly with others about negative thinking, anger, and fear, what I heard was consistent with everything I'd read: *We all struggle!* We all have negative thoughts and reactions we want to change. The question is how? How do you change?

Each person's journey of discovery is unique. There's no single formula or path. But as I explored the experiences of others and reflected on my own, I began to see how these experiences affected their thinking. I started to see patterns, common threads woven through every story, every book, every breakthrough.

I began to see a picture of what every author had been trying to help me understand. Over time, I connected these insights into a framework that showed me the problem and made real transformation possible. I call it **The Reaction Cascade**.

Recognizing the belief systems we've built—and how they shape our perceptions and actions—is essential for personal growth. By better understanding the 'why' behind how we think and act, we can begin challenging our own assumptions and preconceived notions and opening ourselves up to new perspectives and possibilities.

Let's walk through The Reaction Cascade so you can see how the problem manifests and perpetuates our struggles.

Here's the picture I began to see: **We've all been wounded.** And no matter what the experience was, *if it felt traumatic to us*, we seem to have internalized it in a similar way—forming **two powerful foundational beliefs** that serve as the basis for all our other self-perceptions. And these two foundational beliefs sit in what I call the eye of the storm:

Anytime one of the foundational beliefs is triggered by an event, by something that happens, something someone says, or something someone does that causes the thought "I'm not good enough or I'm not worthy," **fear gets ignited**. We don't realize it, however, because it happens instantly.

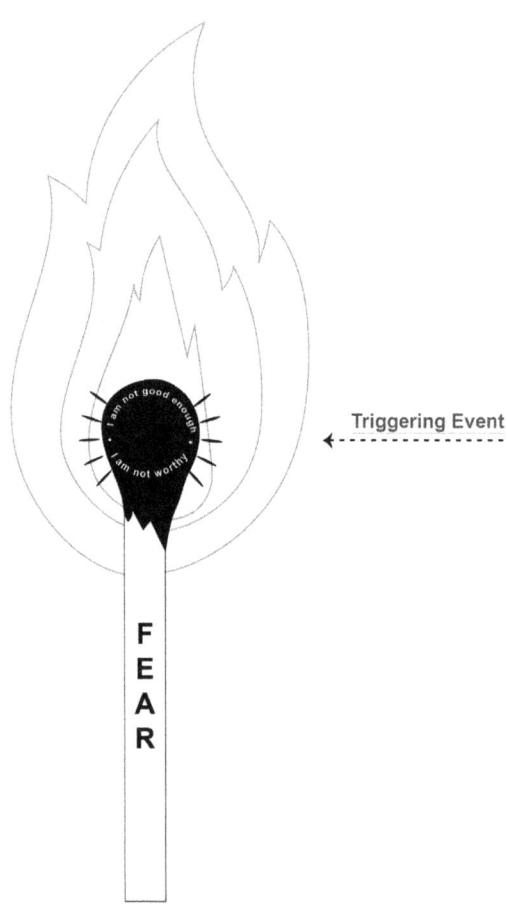

Fear is in our mind. Similar to the two foundational beliefs, the work by Tony Robbins helped me understand that there are three primary fears that serve as the root for all others: Loss, Less, Never.

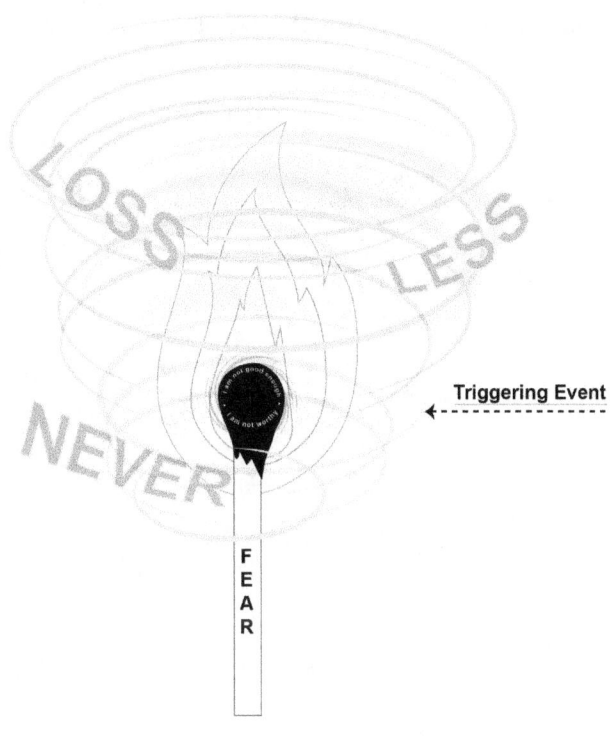

LOSS
Fear of losing what we have

LESS
Fear of being or getting less than what we desire

NEVER
Fear of never getting what we want

Once fear is triggered, it fuels self-centered thinking next. Not in an egotistical way, but in a way that is solely concerned with or absorbed by our own desires, needs, or interests.

Fear triggers self-centered thinking in two ways.

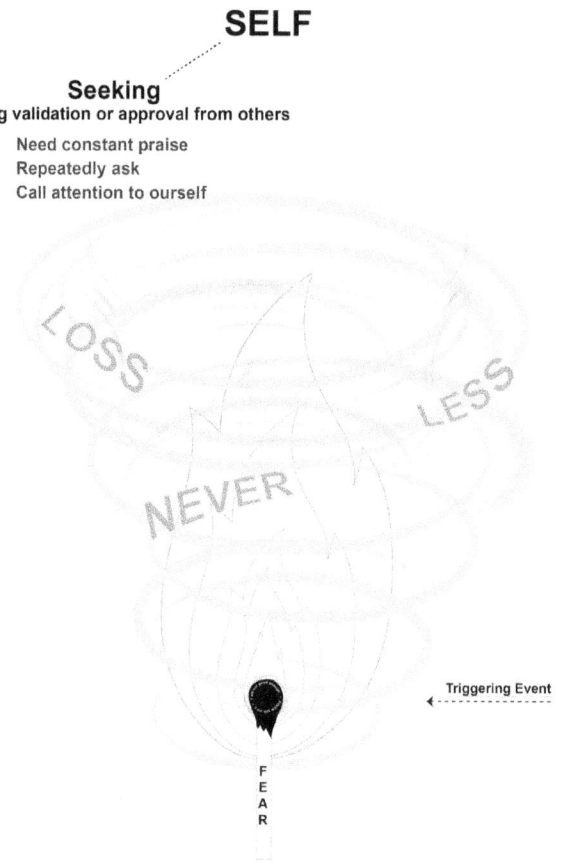

1. Self-seeking

The first is that **our thinking becomes absorbed with needing validation or approval from others.** When we're consumed with needing constant validation or approval, we may repeatedly and often ask our spouse or significant other, "Do you love me?" "Are you happy with me?" You may call attention to yourself by regularly asking if you look okay, etc. Self-seeking carries over at work too, where you not only call attention to your appearance, but you call attention to your contributions, you ask incessantly if you are doing things correctly, you take all the credit for team projects, or you excessively promote yourself during meetings or performance reviews.

In either scenario, the challenge we face when we're self-seeking is that this behavior creates distance. At home, we may create frustration, and at work, we may create distrust. Both lead to distance in our relationships.

2. Self-"ish"

The second way fear affects our thinking is that **we become absorbed with our own needs and desires without considering the impact on others.** And I get it—hearing that our thinking is selfish is hard to accept. In this use, selfish is not the casual description that we're not giving or thoughtful. In this context, the prefix "self" merely means expressing reflective action on or to one's self and to one's own detriment. The behavior or action that follows the word self is the "ish," because it describes what behavior, thought, or feeling we are consumed by which often creates communication barriers or understanding.

Let's unpack each "ish" in the diagram to better understand this concept.

First up is self-avoidance. Avoidance follows the word self; therefore, **avoidance is the "ish."** Self-avoidance is a behavior driven by thinking about the need to escape discomfort, pain, or difficult emotions. When consumed by the avoidance "ish," you may often find yourself thinking or saying, "I'm not dealing with this" or "I need to get out of here," and leave a situation or remain voiceless in it.

Next is self-righteous. **Righteous is the "ish."** Self-righteousness is a negative thought referring to the belief that your morals are superior to others. You may find yourself judging others and often thinking they're wrong or that your way is the only right way. You may feel misunderstood or at odds with people because achieving understanding with another is often difficult when you're consumed by being right all the time.

Finally, self-pity. **Pity is the "ish."** Self-pity is a feeling of sadness and remorse and often involves negative thinking about yourself and your circumstances. When stuck in self-pity, you may constantly voice negativity, despite others' efforts to uplift you. Over time, friends and family might distance themselves, not out of abandonment, but because they feel just as helpless as you and are waiting for you to shift your outlook.

Note: For a more extensive list of "ishes," refer to the Resources section at the back of this book.

Self-seeking and "ish" thinking feed our actions and behavior. And what follows are the actions and behaviors the outside world experiences. We call them **the "Acts."**

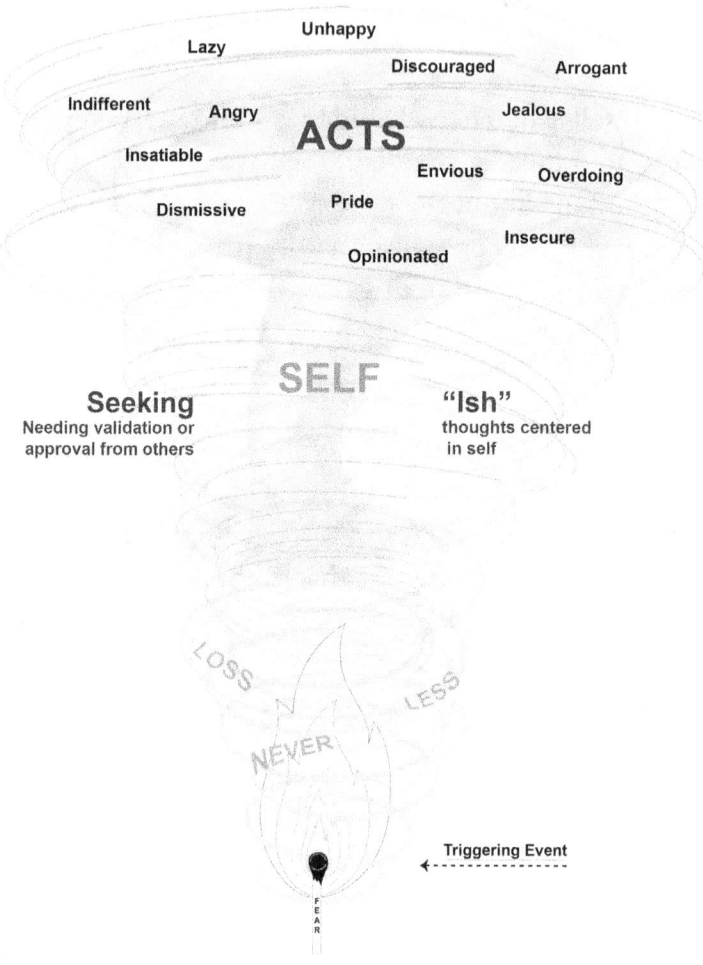

As you look at the Reaction Cascade, examine how a triggering event sparks a limiting belief, ignites fear, then fear fuels self-centered (seeking and "ish") thinking, followed by self-centered thinking feeding the "acts." The "acts" represent how our behavior—fed by our thinking and what we may not see in ourselves—is perceived and experienced by others.

Why does this matter? We all have moments in life when we feel misunderstood and want to give up and scream, "Why does this keep happening to me?" when things aren't going as we'd hoped or planned. And many of us have the tendency to focus on our wounds and the person responsible for them as the reason why. We rehash the past and fight over what really happened. We point our finger away from ourselves toward others. We blame. But does any of this foster connection and fulfillment?

No.

Self-centered thinking blinds us from being able to see ourselves and understand how our "acts" impact others.

The "acts" can create an invisible barrier between you and others, pushing people away through behaviors that dismiss their thoughts and emotions, leaving them feeling unseen and misunderstood. When you're stuck in self-centered thinking, you may be perceived as thoughtless, demanding, defensive, or difficult, making interactions with you draining. Over time, your acts often erode connections, leaving you feeling alone and disconnected.

To establish and maintain strong, meaningful connections, it's essential to recognize and redirect negative thought patterns before they dictate how you engage with others. The challenge? It's not easy for us to see.

Let's explore how some of the "ishes" feed the "acts" and examine how they may sound and what people outside of us may see or how they may experience us:

Example 1: Self-seeking

Self-Centered Thought	>	Things you might say or do	>	Acts people see or how they experience you
Self-seeking	>	Do you love me? Are you happy?	>	Insecure
		Did I do it right?		Not confident
		Oh, **I** did that.		Not trustworthy

Self-seeking may not seem demanding or boastful to us, but to others, it often does. We may believe our spouse doesn't care, our boss is uncommunicative, or that people simply don't recognize our efforts. However, what others see is someone who appears insecure, craves attention, and repeatedly seeks validation, leading to frustration.

In the workplace, self-seeking can come across as trying to undermine others or take undue credit, causing distrust among coworkers.

Can you see how this behavior can be emotionally exhausting for others and why they might distance themselves from you?

Example 2: Self-condemnation

Self-condemnation	>	It's all my fault.	>	Perfectionist
		I'm so stupid.		Dismissive of compliments
		I'll never…		Discouraged and negative

Self-condemnation may seem like a personal struggle, but it affects those around us as well. Constantly apologizing or putting yourself down shifts the focus onto you, prompting reassurance from others like "You don't need to apologize so much" or "Don't be so hard on yourself." Rejecting positive reassurance through self-criticism can feel dismissive and emotionally draining, often creating distance and leaving others feeling unheard, frustrated, or powerless to help you. Can you now see how this behavior creates distance?

Example 3: Self-effacing

Self-effacing	>	It's okay. I don't want to rock the boat or make waves.	>	Avoiding conflict or not advocating for yourself
		Oh, it wasn't a big deal. Anyone could have done it.		Modest, uncomfortable, and embarrassed receiving praise
		I have to take care of…		Putting other's needs first at the expense of your own.

When we're self-effacing, we may appear modest and polite, but we risk losing ourselves by constantly prioritizing others' needs over our own to avoid conflict. While we might not see it as straining relationships, our struggling to accept compliments, deflecting praise, or avoiding expressing our needs can make open and equal communication difficult. Minimizing ourselves can unintentionally create emotional distance, leaving others feeling unheard or dismissed.

Can you see how this behavior can lead to frustration or fatigue in the relationship?

Example 4: Self-reliance

Self-Reliance	>	I don't need any help. I can handle this on my own.	>	Lone Wolf, isolated
		I have to do it, because only I can get it done right.		Perfectionist
		If you want something done right, you have to do it yourself.		Overcommitted, stressed

Self-reliance is valuable during adolescence as we strive for independence, but in adulthood, this "ish" can create emotional distance in relationships. The belief that we must handle everything ourselves, paired with a reluctance to ask for help or share vulnerabilities, can make us seem overcommitted, emotionally unavailable, or even unapproachable. Others may begin to see us as perfectionists who don't need or trust their support, leaving them feeling unneeded, unappreciated, or shut out.

Can you see how self-reliance erodes connection?

Your struggles—the Reaction Cascade—start within you.

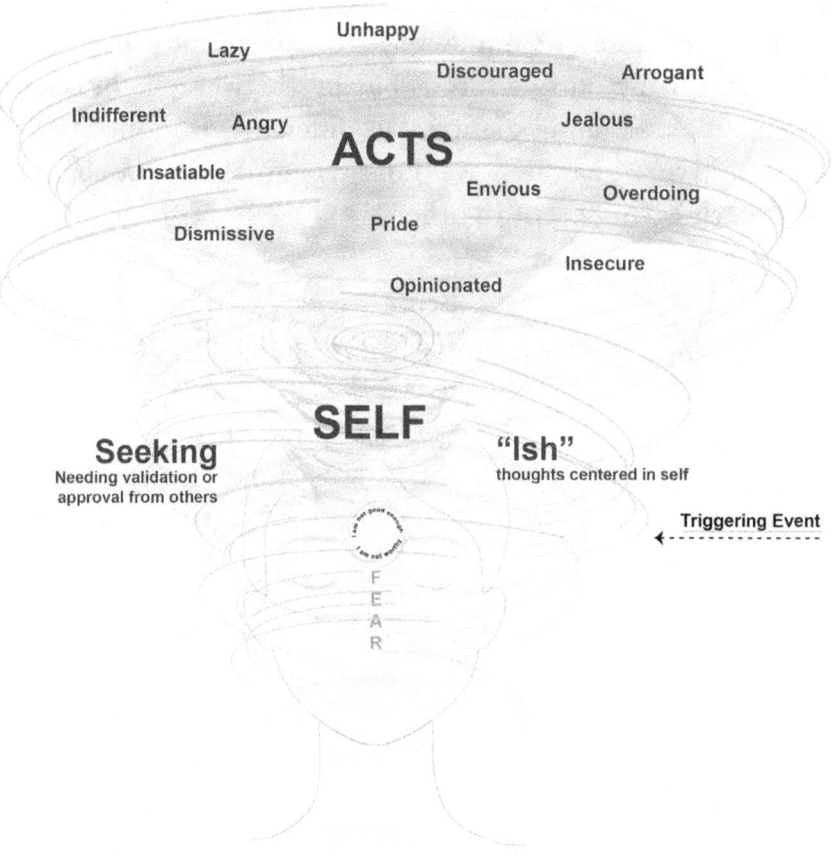

Can you now see how your struggle with others starts within you? The storm starts when fear is ignited by the belief that we're not good enough or worthy. Fear fuels the storm further with seeking and "ish" thinking, which feeds how we act and how we affect others.

Our Storms Trigger Others

Like the 'mitote' Ruiz talks about, we're unable to see who we really are because our minds stay stuck in the storm. We're all blocked, not by outside forces, but by the way we think. And when people see and experience us differently from how we see ourselves, we're unaware—**we don't recognize how we act may be the triggering event in others.**

And what happens when others are triggered? Misunderstandings. No one can identify with or understand another's experience. We get trapped inside of our minds and pull away.

We all have inner storms that block us from attaining meaningful connection, which make us unable to truly give or receive understanding.

Our thinking and actions repel. We seek to draw people closer when we're really pushing them away. We think we're doing the right thing by not rocking the boat, but we seem detached and uncaring. We think we're speaking up for ourselves, but we appear judgmental, impatient, or dismissive. We think love is managing it all. Then we think we're a burden when people try to love us. We often feel misunderstood, yet we rarely make the effort to understand others. In truth, we're all disconnected—lost in our own storms, like magnets repelling each other.

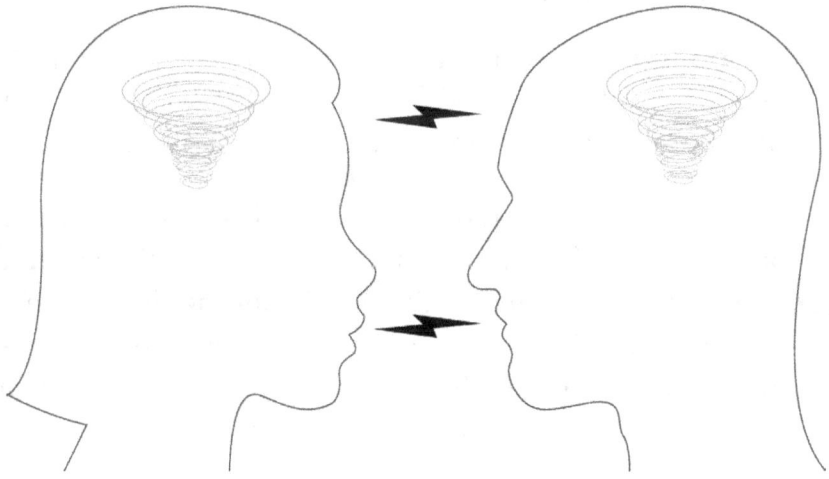

The real question is, how do we regain connection? How do we attract rather than repel?

The journey to clear skies begins with a shift in perspective. We often say we forgive, yet we hold on to the past. To truly overcome our struggles, we must break free from self-centered thinking and recognize the impact our thinking and acts have on others.

We must be willing to let go of old ideas. After all, where has our best thinking led us? Too often, it leaves us alone, disconnected, and unfulfilled. We need to break through our resistance to change. Most of us say we want to grow, yet we remain stuck in our storms simply because they feel familiar. They're safe, predictable, and easy to explain. It's change that scares us.

But change doesn't happen without action.

Change Begins with the Aurora Method

The Aurora Method was inspired by several influences in my life. The foundation of the method follows that of the great psychologist, Abraham Maslow, and the great psychiatrist, M. Scott Peck.

Maslow believed that trauma or difficult circumstances at a point in time of a person's life may stunt their personal growth and development. His model explains that personal growth may be stalled when basic emotional and psychological needs—like emotional and financial security, belonging, esteem, and fulfilling our own potential—are disrupted.

By recognizing which needs were stunted and uncovering the beliefs and fear formed in response, we gain the power to change. This awareness empowers us to recognize and redirect self-seeking and "ish" thinking, freeing us from anger, discontentment, fear, and negativity.

Peck believed that life is difficult and challenging and that emotional and spiritual growth often comes through suffering and confronting painful truths rather than avoiding them. His writings teach that **accepting hardship and emotional pain makes it easier to navigate life's storms with resilience.**

The first step of the Aurora Method is self-assessment, an honest—and at times painful—reflection on the life experiences that have wounded and shaped you. This tool was inspired from the book *Alcoholics Anonymous*. This self-assessment asks us to go beyond blame. It challenges us to rethink why, and it pushes us to rise above the storm clouds and look honestly at ourselves. This is your foundational tool.

What follows is The Turnaround, a tool inspired by Carl Jung, comprising exercises that will help you see yourself from a different perspective, essentially connecting the conscious and unconscious mind, *so that you can make a complete turnaround in your thinking.*

The remaining Aurora Method tools and practices align with the teachings of great spiritual leaders, emphasizing that forgiveness, acceptance, understanding, kindness, and love are the keys to solving our struggles. Personal and spiritual growth is a lifelong journey, one that requires daily discipline, self-awareness, openness to change, a willingness to grow, and a deep commitment to the grace that helps us transcend our limitations and achieve personal transformation.

The Aurora Method is designed to illuminate how your life experiences have shaped your thinking and guide you toward meaningful change. It helps you nurture love, strengthen relationships, and grow both personally and professionally. By recognizing and redirecting self-centered thoughts, you'll learn to navigate life's daily storms with greater clarity. Ultimately, the Aurora Method helps you strengthen your connection with yourself and others and develop the power within you, fostering continuous personal growth.

> "If you're going to be truthful with yourself, you have to be honest. And if you're going to be honest, you have to be truthful."
>
> —Augustus Edward Doyle Sr. (Pop)

Embracing the Waves of Change

The Self-Assessment

Have you ever:

- ☼ Felt like you weren't being heard, had trouble taking a deep breath, and become noticeably frustrated?
- ☼ Reacted to someone where your reaction made you feel guilty, ashamed, or remorseful?
- ☼ Found yourself complaining to your friends, family, or co-workers about the sorry state of your life? Your job? Your relationship? Your boss?

Have you ever:

- ☼ Gone out of your way to help someone or exceeded expectations at home or work, and it went unacknowledged, leaving you feeling undervalued and filled with anger?
- ☼ Tried hard to make things better for *them*, only for things to get worse for you, leaving you feeling unappreciated and misunderstood?
- ☼ Found yourself thinking that life and the people in it are treating you unfairly?

If you found yourself saying "yes" to any of these questions, chances are you are caught in the Reaction Cascade and seeing life through the lens of lack, discontentment, and past wounds. It's a pattern that keeps us stuck, repeating the same struggles, waiting for external circumstances to change instead of shifting our own perspective.

We've all been wounded by the words or actions of others, and those wounds shape us. Perhaps a parent or teacher constantly criticized you, leaving you feeling inadequate, or childhood taunting made you doubt your worth. Maybe a friend betrayed your trust through gossip, or a loved one let you down in ways that still linger. And some wounds run even deeper; traumatic experiences like physical, sexual, or emotional abuse can leave lasting scars.

Whatever the source, *our wounds matter.* These experiences create two foundational beliefs and three primary fears which distort how we see ourselves and navigate our relationships. Our wounds limit us because they hold us back from that sense of connection we often crave and create barriers leaving us feeling inept and misunderstood. They leave lasting feelings of anger and futility. They steal our joy.

If you're struggling in your relationships at home or at work and you're longing to reconnect and find joy in your life, are you willing to take the necessary steps to improve them? Change is hard. It takes work. And a commitment.

I'm sure you've adopted things you've learned along the way. And over time, it seems things went back to how they were, and you were left feeling dejected, discontented, irritated, and discouraged, thinking, *nothing works.* But if you get honest with yourself, you'll likely discover that you've been uncertain and afraid of change—you're resistant.

On my own journey, my fear-based thinking tried to convince me that it's not worth the effort. I found myself playing a fierce game of Ping-Pong in my mind. On the one side, I was saying, "*Are things really that bad? Do I really need to do this? No, things are fine.*" Whereas, on the other side, I was saying, "*I can't take it anymore. How do I fix this? How can I make this better?*"

For me, real change required letting go of old beliefs. I had to open my mind and embrace a new approach. I had to be willing to get honest with myself and do what it takes—every day. And when fear and doubt crept in, I had to, like Susan Jeffers said, "feel the fear and do it anyway."

Through the Aurora Method, I experienced real and lasting change.

I discovered I *was* able to change my perspective. In most cases, I was able to forgive those who had wounded me. But more importantly, I became aware of how my negative thinking perpetuated problems and, specifically, what self-centered thinking and behavior needed to change. In other words, when something was said or done that triggered my Reaction Cascade, rather than always having an emotional outburst, I gained an approach which allowed me to stop the internal storm, think it through, and redirect my thinking.

And it didn't stop there!

All the great spiritual teachers dating back millenniums and psychology educators alike seem to tell us one consistent message:

To change, we must become aware. Once aware, we must remain vigilant. And to stay vigilant, we must practice. Like the athlete seeking to be the best they can be, practice must be daily. Real and lasting change requires commitment.

How we practice becomes our life's journey of emotional healing and connection.

I'm excited to share the Aurora Method with you, as these tools have been pivotal in helping me improve my own life.

Approach the self-assessment with an open mind. Trust the process and choose to follow through with it. No matter what. And above all else, be honest with yourself. Approach the exercise with a non-critical attitude. The assessment isn't intended to make you feel bad about yourself or others. It's a practical tool to help you see what's holding you back, so you know what and how to change.

The self-assessment may be enlightening. You might experience a few "AHAs" about yourself.

And if you're like me, you might be tempted to stop there. But I urge you to continue and heed the advice of the great teachers. With daily practice, you'll start to intuitively identify your seeking and "ish" thinking and recognize which fear has been ignited. You'll understand what's happening amid the storm and know how to navigate your way out to your clear sky.

Are you ready? Let's get busy!

The Self-Assessment

The purpose of the self-assessment is to help you identify how your life experiences shaped your thinking. This is your foundational step for the Aurora Method journey.

How to Get Started:
- ☼ Download and print the Self-Assessment at www.tracydoyle.life/Resources.
  The Self-Assessment Worksheet is also at the end of this book in the Resources Section.
- ☼ Begin in the first column, then go column by column, completing each one before moving to the next.
- ☼ Don't overthink it. List only what comes to the surface quickly.

Let's complete the Self-Assessment

Column 1: Who am I angry with or who has hurt me?

Reflect on each decade of your life. Who were you angry with or who hurt you before the age of ten? In your twenties? Between the ages thirty and forty? In your forties? Over fifty?

As you reflect on each period, list each person who comes to mind, putting them into a separate row.

Tip: It's okay to write the same person's name more than once.

You don't have to do this alone. Visit www.tracydoyle.life if you need help.

Column 2: What did they do?

Describe the hurt or the thing done to cause the hurt or anger in one to two sentences. Keep it short and simple. The idea is to review one general thing or theme. See the example for context.

Tips: If the person did several things that hurt or angered you, reflecting separate issues, list them separately. Put their name in column 1 again, then write what they did in column 2. You may have a whole sheet for one person! It's okay. The idea is to have a single memory in column 2. Refer to the example for context.

Columns 1 & 2: Example from my Self-Assessment

Who am I angry with? Who hurt me?	What did they do?
Uncle	Molested me on more than one occasion
Nanny	Called me a bastard and made me sit on the floor
Stepfather	Left us home alone. Didn't pay bills or provide food
Mom	Banged my head repeatedly on the table when I couldn't understand fractions
Mom	Didn't help me when I told her about being molested and wanted me to tell her what to do

 Stop and reflect.

When you've finished, ask yourself, "Is it complete?" Go back to each point in time and ask the questions

---

You don't have to do this alone. Visit www.tracydoyle.life if you need help.

again. If someone or something immediately comes to the surface, add it, regardless of whether you think it is unnecessary or not. Just do it and trust the process.

Column 3: How did this affect me?

This column helps you recognize how your life experiences have affected you and is an adaptation of Maslow's Hierarchy of Needs. Remember, Maslow believed that trauma or emotional wounds experienced at any point in a person's life could impact their basic emotional needs, therefore stunting personal growth and development.

Before we start, let's review the basic needs according to Maslow:

- ☼ **Safety and Financial Security,** or our need to feel safe and protected in our environment or secure related to our material well-being (food, shelter, clothes, etc).

- ☼ **Social Belonging,** or our need for friendships, family connections, and intimacy with others.

Column 3 separates social belonging into three separate areas: emotional security (well-being overall), personal relations (acceptance by family, friends, significant others), and intimate relations (safe and secure in intimate relationships).

- ☼ **Esteem,** or the need for being liked and respected by others and self-respect for oneself.

- ☼ **Self-Actualization,** or needs related to fulfilling your own potential or ambitions across areas that are personally important to you (column 3 lists this as "Ambitions").

You don't have to do this alone. Visit www.tracydoyle.life if you need help.

Why is it important to understand which needs were impacted?

Maslow believed that, when our needs are handicapped, we may live in a state of discontent or lack. For example, if our emotional security or esteem is stunted, we may internalize it as not being good enough and fear losing what we have. In turn, we become self-seeking, demanding constant validation and approval from our spouse, family, or friends. On the other hand, if our safety and financial security are stunted, we may live in fear that we aren't safe, despite living in a safe neighborhood or incessantly worry that we won't have enough money, when we have more than enough. Maslow believed that being stuck on a specific set of needs could be the root cause of many problems affecting a person's well-being and happiness.

Now let's complete column 3, "How did this affect me?"

To understand what was affected, you'll look to column 2 (What did they do?). For every "Who" and "What," ask yourself, *"How did this affect me?"*

To answer the question, refer to the reflection questions provided for each need. When you answer "yes" to any of the questions related to a particular need, place an "x" in the corresponding box.

Tip: It's okay if you place an "x" in more than one box. See my example for context. If you need help with what each need means, see the Resources section at the back of the book.

You don't have to do this alone. Visit www.tracydoyle.life if you need help.

Reflection Questions:

Safety and Financial Security:
- ☼ Did this affect how safe I felt in my surroundings? Did I feel unprotected?
- ☼ Did I feel deprived or that I wouldn't have a place to live, food to eat, or clothes to wear?

Emotional Security:
- ☼ Did I feel unsafe? Unloved? Unsupported or uncared for?
- ☼ Did I feel unsure or confused?

Personal Relations:
- ☼ Did I feel like I didn't fit in or belong? Rejected?
- ☼ Did I feel distrustful of family or friends?

Intimate Relations:
- ☼ Did I feel threatened by or distrustful of men or women?
- ☼ Did I feel bad about my sexuality?

Esteem:
- ☼ Did this affect how I felt about myself (e.g., "I'm bad," "I'm not good enough")?
- ☼ Did I feel unliked? Unheard? Unacknowledged? Taken for granted?

Ambitions:
- ☼ Did I feel that I wouldn't be able to achieve what I want for myself?
- ☼ Did I feel like I would be a failure and would never get what I want?

You don't have to do this alone. Visit www.tracydoyle.life if you need help.

Column 3: Example from my Self-Assessment

Who...?	What...?	How did this affect me?					
		Safety & Financial Security	Emotional Security	Personal Relations	Intimate Relations	Esteem	Ambitions
Uncle	...	X	X	X	X	X	X
Nanny	...		X	X		X	X

Column 4: What did I do?

Now let's look at your reactions to the injustices and harm done. This part of the exercise asks you to be truthful and honest with yourself about how you acted in response to the person. It's essential to be detailed about your actions, as you'll gain insight into what needs to change later.

Start at the top and move down the list. Ask yourself the reflection questions and describe how you responded to what happened using two to three sentences. See my example for context.

Reflection Questions:

- ☼ What did I do or say to the person? Did I retaliate or act out? How?
- ☼ Did I fight or argue? What unkind things did I say or do?
- ☼ Did I avoid or abandon? How? What didn't I say or do?
- ☼ Did I seek comfort outside of myself to get back at the person and to feel good about myself? What did I do? (drink alcohol, eat, have sex, spend money, etc.)
- ☼ Did I try to be invisible? Remain silent or ignore the person? What negative things did I say to myself?

You don't have to do this alone. Visit www.tracydoyle.life if you need help.

Column 4: Example from my Self-Assessment

Who…?	What..?	How…?	What Did I Do?
Uncle	…	…	I remained silent and pretended like nothing happened. I asked God why he would let this happen to me.
Nanny	…	…	I avoided/ignored her and lied to her when she asked me questions about my mom. I pretended everything was alright.

Is it complete? Review the reflection questions and your answers. Were you honest? Accurate? Did you downplay anything? Make sure you accurately capture your actions or thoughts in response to the harm or injustice. The information you provide here will help guide you later.

 ## Consider Taking a Break

This is hard work, and your well-being is worth all your effort!

This next section will take a lot of reflection and time. It may feel tedious and repetitive, and at times, you may just feel like checking all the boxes. I urge you to take your time, as this last step in the Self-Assessment is the most important.

Before you get started, be sure to familiarize yourself with the "ish" definitions in the Resources Section at the back of this book or you can download them at www.tracydoyle.life/Resources.

You don't have to do this alone. Visit www.tracydoyle.life if you need help.

You'll likely find yourself referring to them often as you reflect on each listed hurt or anger and answer the accompanying questions.

Starting this column fresh is always best. I suggest you pause, rest, and then revisit this next section tomorrow.

Column 5: Examine your actions.

Approach this next step by momentarily setting aside what others have done to you and take an honest look at your own actions. We're examining five areas: seeking and "ish" thinking, honesty with ourselves and others, the ability to consider another's feelings, and fear (see chart).

What Did I Do?	Was I ...				
	Self-Seeking	Self-"ish"	Dishonest	Thoughtless	Afraid
...					

 Don't skip this step!

It may tire you out. But don't stop! You may feel resistant. Walls may try to come up. Overcome the fight in your head to proceed. You might try to convince yourself that it isn't necessary, but it is. This step is critical in helping you identify your blocks.

Remember, your goal is to break through and gain clarity on your Reaction Cascade, so you can restore connection and fulfillment in your personal and professional relationships. This is how you'll gain the insight you need to do it. You'll open yourself up to a whole new perspective and make self-improvement possible. Resist the fight, and *just do it*!

You don't have to do this alone. Visit www.tracydoyle.life if you need help.

Familiarize Yourself with the "ish" Definitions

Take a moment to read and reflect on them. You may need to ask yourself the same questions more than once to uncover deeper insights and move toward your clear sky. The more familiar you are with them, the better. If you haven't downloaded them, it may be helpful to go to www.tracydoyle.life/Resources to print them out and have them nearby.

Once you're ready, let's begin:

- ☼ Review "What did I do?" (column 4) only. Don't look at the name of the person in column 1 or what they did in column 2.
- ☼ Review each set of reflection questions, and when you answer "yes," place an "x" in each corresponding box.
- ☼ The "ish" section is critical. As you go through each hurt/anger, you'll be asked to jot down the specific code for each "ish" identified. The definitions are found in the Resources Section at the back of the book or you can download them at www.tracydoyle.life/Resources.
- ☼ In the fear section, you'll be asked to note which primary fear(s) were identified: Loss, Less, or Never.

If you need help, see my example for context. You can also go to www.tracydoyle.life to learn how I can support you further.

You may find yourself answering "yes" often to certain questions. Whereas for others, you may not. That's okay. Just be as honest and as thorough as possible.

You don't have to do this alone. Visit www.tracydoyle.life if you need help.

Reflection Questions:

Look at Column 4 and ask: Was I Self-Seeking?
If you answer "yes" to any of these questions, place an "x" in the box:

- ☼ Did I expect recognition, praise, or attention and become upset when I didn't get it?
- ☼ Did I brag or point out what I did or said to get attention?
- ☼ Did I repeatedly ask if what I'm doing is okay or if they like or love me and become upset because I had to ask?
- ☼ Did I seek comfort outside of myself when I didn't get the validation I wanted?

Look at Column 4 and ask: Was I Self-"ish"?
All of the questions that follow are related to the second column titled self-"ish." When you've identified "ish" thinking, simply place an "x," then add the specific code associated with the "ish." You may identify more than one "ish" for each hurt/anger you're examining. It's okay to add as many as you find. You'll benefit from this effort later.

If you're stuck, see the example from my Self-Assessment for context.

You don't have to do this alone. Visit www.tracydoyle.life if you need help.

The "Ish" Reflection Questions:

The "Ish"	*While looking at Column 4 ask:*
Self-Avoidance (A):	Did I avoid dealing with the person/situation by isolating or busying myself? Did I escape my feelings by numbing with alcohol, food, shopping, etc? If yes, add (A).
Self-Condemnation (C):	Did I blame myself, think it was all my fault, or put myself down? If yes, add (C).
Self-Deception (DEC):	Did I convince myself that what I did was okay? Did I know what I did was wrong and lie to myself about it? If yes, add (DEC).
Self-Deprecation (DEP):	Did I beat myself up or criticize myself for what I did? If yes, add (DEP).
Self-Doubt (D):	Was I afraid or unable to take action? Or was I really hard on myself about my abilities? If yes, add (D).
Self-Effacing (E):	Did I remain silent or try to deflect? Did I redirect attention and praise? If yes, add (E).
Self-Importance (I):	Did I try to show them how important or smart I am? Was I arrogant, condescending, impatient, or dismissive? If yes, add (I).
Self-Justification (J):	Did I finger point and blame or become defensive? Did I rationalize my actions, even though I knew they were wrong? If yes, add (J).

You don't have to do this alone. Visit www.tracydoyle.life if you need help.

Self-Loathing (L):	Did I feel like a failure or inept? Did I say negative things to myself and believe that no matter what I do, I'll never be good enough? If yes, add (L)
Self-Pity (P):	Did I act like a victim or feel sorry for myself? Did I say to myself that no one understands, cares, loves, or appreciates me? If yes, add (P).
Self-Reliance (RE):	Did I overcommit or do everything myself and not ask for help? Did I say to myself, "I'm the only one who can do it because I can't rely on anyone," or "I have to do because I want it done right?" If yes, add (RE).
Self-Righteous (RI):	Did I act like my way was the only right way or engage in a who-is-right fight, insisting that my way or opinion is best, regardless of what the person thought? If yes, add (RI).

Look at Column 4 and ask: Was I Dishonest?

Did I intentionally lie, or did I lie through omission ("They didn't ask, so I'm not saying anything")? If yes, place an "x" in the dishonest box.

You don't have to do this alone. Visit www.tracydoyle.life if you need help.

Look at Column 4 and ask: Was I Thoughtless?
Was I unkind or inconsiderate? Dismissive? Arrogant? Purposely disregarding the other person's feelings because of what they'd done to me? Did I act and not think about how the other person might feel? If yes, place an "x" in the thoughtless box.

Look at Column 4 and ask: Was I Afraid?
If yes, which fear did you feel? Place an "x" in the box and note the fear(s): "Loss," "Less," or "Never."

☼ **Loss:** I was afraid of losing what I have.
☼ **Less:** I was afraid of being or getting less than I desire.
☼ **Never:** I was afraid I would never get what I want.

Column 5: Example from my Self-Assessment

What Did I Do?	Was I …				
	Self-Seeking	Self-"ish"	Dishonest	Thought-less	Afraid
…	X	X P, C, E	X		X Loss Never
		X P, E	X		X Loss

Once you're done with this step, you've finished your self-assessment!

CONGRATULATIONS!

You don't have to do this alone. Visit www.tracydoyle.life if you need help.

Take Another Break

You've worked hard. Plan on taking a break for a day or two. It's important that you approach the next exercise, The Turnaround, rested and refreshed because you're going to learn a lot.

The purpose of The Turnaround is to help you identify how your self-centered thinking and actions affect others. There are several steps to complete. Each step will help you gain insight and knowledge about yourself with the aim of helping you discover what needs to change.

When you're ready, move to the next chapter and complete The Turnaround!

"When we are no longer able to change a situation, we are challenged to change ourselves."

—Viktor Frankl

Emerging from the Fog
The Turnaround

The next step of the Aurora Method is The Turnaround, or the ability to change your perspective.

I'm sure you're wondering, "What am I really getting from doing all this?" If you're anything like me, you may be searching for the label so you can say, "Yep, that's me. That's what's wrong with me. Now I know!" But remember, we're not here to diagnose or label! There are professionals trained for that.

What you're gaining is the ability to identify how your life experiences have shaped your thinking and how your thinking is affecting you and your relationships. With this knowledge, you can shift your perspective and apply your insight to change and improve your outlook and the relationships in your life.

The Turnaround

How to Get Started:

- ☼ Download and print The Turnaround at www.tracydoyle.life/Resources. The Worksheet can also be found at the back of this book in the Resources Section.
- ☼ You'll need your completed Self-Assessment. This is a prerequisite. If you skipped ahead, go back and finish up.
- ☼ Be sure to have your journal handy, as you may want to write about some of your "AHAs."

Identify What Needs Have Been Stunted

Review "How did this affect me?" (column 3) on your completed Self-Assessment:

- ☼ Do you see any patterns?
- ☼ What needs are checked off repeatedly or consistently (eight times or greater)?
- ☼ Looking at your patterns, what do you see about yourself?

After your review:

- ☼ Note on The Turnaround only those needs that were checked most consistently on the Self-Assessment (eight times or greater).
- ☼ Briefly write what you see or have learned about yourself. Refer to the example.

You don't have to do this alone. Visit www.tracydoyle.life if you need help.

My Needs: Example from my Turnaround

The Turnaround
How did my life experiences affect me? (Check all that apply) × Safety and financial security were threatened. × Emotional security was threatened. × Social belonging related to relationships with others was threatened. × Social belonging related to relationships with love interests was threatened. × Social belonging related to my being liked by others and myself was threatened. × Ambitions were threatened.
Looking at your need patterns, what do you see about yourself?
I'm threatened and insecure in matters concerning money and personal relationships. My sense of belonging was severely stunted. I don't trust men or women at all. I don't value myself and am not confident in my abilities. I'm filled with self-doubt. What I wanted for myself academically and professionally was affected badly; I became an overachiever.

This exercise helped me to quickly see how my life experiences deeply affected me. Although I had been to therapy, I hadn't quite internalized how I was stunted. But I could now see what my therapist saw. I needed emotional healing.

You don't have to do this alone. Visit www.tracydoyle.life if you need help.

Identify Your Primary Fears

Review "Examine your actions" (column 5) on your completed Self-Assessment:

- ☼ Do you see any patterns?
- ☼ What fears ("Loss," "Less," "Never") are noted repeatedly and consistently (eight times or greater)?
- ☼ What do you do most often in the presence of fear? Are you thoughtless? Dishonest?

After your review:

- ☼ Note on The Turnaround only the primary fears that were noted most consistently on the Self-Assessment. It's okay if they were all noted consistently. (See example.)
- ☼ Looking at each fear, examine which behavior (thoughtless or dishonest) was checked off most often. For example, if you identified a "Less" fear, assess all your sheets and determine which behavior was most prominent: dishonest or thoughtless?
- ☼ Note the most prominent behavior associated with each fear. (See example.)

You don't have to do this alone. Visit www.tracydoyle.life if you need help.

My Fears: Example from my Turnaround

The Turnaround My Fear Patterns
How have my life experiences affected fear? Looking at your fear patterns, what are your primary fears? (Select the fears that were most consistently noted on your Self-Assessment. It's okay if all three were selected equally.) ✓ LOSS: Fear of losing what we have What do you do most in the presence of this fear? (check one) ✓   I am thoughtless. I don't think about how my actions affect others. ☐   I am dishonest. I outright tell a lie or I lie by omission (not saying anything at all). ✓ LESS: Fear of being or getting less than we desire What do you do most in the presence of this fear? (check one) ☐   I am thoughtless. I don't think about how my actions affect others. ✓   I am dishonest. I outright tell a lie or I lie by omission (not saying anything at all). ✓ NEVER: Fear of never getting what we want What do you do most in the presence of this fear? (check one) ✓   I am thoughtless. I don't think about how my actions affect others. ☐   I am dishonest. I outright tell a lie or I lie by omission (not saying anything at all).

You don't have to do this alone. Visit www.tracydoyle.life if you need help.

Identify Your Self-centered Thinking Patterns

Review "Examine your actions" (column 5) on your completed Self-Assessment:

- ☼ Do you see any self-centered thinking patterns?
- ☼ What "ishes" were noted repeatedly and consistently (eight times or greater)?

After your review:

- ☼ Note on The Turnaround only the self-centered thinking patterns (seeking and "ishes") that were noted most consistently on the Self-Assessment by placing a check mark in the corresponding box. It's okay if you have many. (See example.)
- ☼ If you identified other "ishes" not provided on The Turnaround, note them under "Other."

You don't have to do this alone. Visit www.tracydoyle.life if you need help.

My Thinking: Example from my Turnaround

The Turnaround My Thinking Patterns	
How does my fear fuel my thinking? Looking at your patterns, what are your primary self-centered thinking patterns? (Select the seeking and "ishes" that were noted as the most consistent on your Self-Assessment.) Note: This exercise is personal to you. Should the "ishes" listed not include an "ish" you've identified, please note it or any others in the 'Other' section.	
☒ Self-avoidance ☐ Self-condemnation ☐ Self-deception ☒ Self-deprecation ☒ Self-doubt ☐ Self-effacing ☒ Self-importance	☐ Self-justification ☐ Self-loathing ☒ Self-pity ☒ Self-reliance ☒ Self-righteous ☒ Self-seeking ☐ Other:

You don't have to do this alone. Visit www.tracydoyle.life if you need help.

Identify Your Behavior Patterns ("The Acts")

Review "Examine your actions" (column 5) and "What did I do?" (column 4) on your completed Self-Assessment:

- ☼ Examine if you've checked off thoughtless or dishonest eight times or more.

- ☼ Review "What did I do?" (column 4). What were the most common behaviors that you see consistently (e.g., anger, frustration, avoidance, envy, gossiping, etc.)?

After your review:

- ☼ Note on The Turnaround only the behavior patterns or "acts" that were noted most consistently on the Self-Assessment by placing a check mark in the corresponding box. It's okay if you have many. (See example.)

- ☼ If you identified other behaviors not provided on The Turnaround, note them under "other."

You don't have to do this alone. Visit www.tracydoyle.life if you need help.

My Behavior: Example from my Turnaround

The Turnaround
My Behavior Patterns
How does my thinking affect my behavior? Looking at your behavior, what are your common behavior patterns? (Select the behavior patterns most consistent as noted on your Self-Assessment.) Note: This exercise is personal to you. Should the "behavior" listed not include something you've identified, please note it or any others in the 'Other' section.

✗	Angry	☐	Indecisive
✗	Argumentative	✗	Isolated
✗	Arrogant	☐	Jealous
☐	Blame	☐	Judgmental
☐	Complain	✗	Negative
✗	Condescending	☐	Noncommitted
✗	Demanding	✗	Opinionated
☐	Defensive	✗	Overcommitted
☐	Dishonest	✗	Prideful
✗	Dismissive	☐	Procrastinate
✗	Envious	☐	Voiceless (didn't speak up)
☐	Gossip		
✗	Impatient	☐	Other:

You don't have to do this alone. Visit www.tracydoyle.life if you need help.

Turn Around Your Thinking

Before we get started let's take a moment to understand why this part of the exercise is important.

Negative emotional reactions are often in response to perceptions of being mistreated.

Self-centered thinking holds you back because it shapes your perception of reality and limits your potential. When you constantly focus on obstacles, setbacks, or worst-case scenarios, your mind reinforces fear, making success seem unattainable because negative thinking repels. However, by learning how to recognize and redirect negative thinking (fear and self-centered thoughts), you open yourself up to possibilities, resilience, and confidence.

Positive thinking attracts opportunities and helps you see challenges as stepping stones rather than roadblocks. When you shift your mindset, you change how you approach life, which ultimately changes your outcomes. Many of us try so hard to shift our mindset, yet we continue to struggle.

Why?

Because our wounds leave scars, and those scars manifest as unresolved resentment.

Resentment comes from the French word *resentir*, where *sentir* means "to feel" or "to experience." **When we *re*-feel or *re*-experience past wounds, we often react in ways that are misaligned with what's happening in the present moment.** What we *re*-experience inside our mind are perceptions of wrongdoing or feelings of injustice that come from past experiences.

You don't have to do this alone. Visit www.tracydoyle.life if you need help.

When we're in this state of mind, we find ourselves feeling blamed or blaming—we point to all the externals as the cause of our anger, discontentment, unhappiness, etc. We often believe, "If only they would do what I want, then everything would be alright," "If only she did what I asked, then I would be happy," "If only I had enough money, then I would be content," or "If they just listened to me and understood what I was trying to say, then I would be calm."

Resentment is a thief. It causes us to *re*-feel a perceived wrong or threat, and it robs us of experiencing joy and harmony in the present moment. It keeps us trapped. As we learned from Maslow, we become stunted and remain absorbed in our life's wrongs. Resentment often holds us back from letting go or forgiving others or ourselves. **Unresolved resentment**, then, often **causes our ongoing struggles and perpetuates emotional burnout.**

Like we learned in the chapter, "Eye of the Storm," when a triggering event sparks the belief that "I'm not good enough" or "I'm not worthy," it ignites fear which fuels the cascade of seeking and "ish" thoughts we're not able to control. We merely act on them, which is the one thing we *can* control.

We can control the "acts" by uncovering what we are *re*-feeling and recognizing how unresolved resentment replays in our lives. **Seeing** perceived injustices trapped in our mind and learning how to redirect our fear and self-centered thinking **is the key to freedom and regaining connection** to the people who matter.

The real shift happens when we realize that inner peace and serenity must come first. When we find peace within ourselves, our perspectives change, our responses change, and in turn, our experience of the world changes.

You don't have to do this alone. Visit www.tracydoyle.life if you need help.

In the previous exercises, you identified the needs that were affected by your life experiences, your fears and how you respond to them, either by dishonesty (flight) or thoughtlessness (fight). And you identified what parts of "self" you become absorbed by (seeking and/or "ishes") and how they feed your behavior ("acts"). Now it's time to turn around the perceived injustices we replay.

The next exercise starts the process of shifting mindset.

Complete Your Turnaround Statements

The goal of this exercise is to help you bring your self-centered thinking into conscious awareness and turn it around so you can begin improving your relationships.

Let's take this step by step:

- ☼ We'll review columns 5, 4, and 3 on your complete Self-Assessment.
- ☼ Start with the first row on the first page and go all the way to the right, to the last column titled "Afraid." We will be reading right to left.
- ☼ What fear(s) did you identify for that row?
- ☼ Now, fill in the blank: When I'm gripped by _____ (loss, less, or never) fear.
- ☼ Read left; do you have thoughtless or dishonest checked off?
- ☼ If so, fill in the next blank: I'm_____ (thoughtless or dishonest).

You don't have to do this alone. Visit www.tracydoyle.life if you need help.

☼ What "ishes" have you identified? Did you select "seeking?"

☼ Fill in the next blank with all that you identified: My thinking is absorbed with_____ ("ishes" and/or seeking).

☼ Now, look at "What did I do?" (column 4) and read how you acted. With the "ish" or seeking in mind, identify the behavior associated with it.

☼ Fill in the blanks: When I'm _____ (ish and/or seeking), I_____ (insert the behavior from column 4).

☼ If you had more than one "ish," following the same steps you just completed, fill in the next two blanks.

☼ Then I _____ (insert the behavior from column 4 and corresponding "ish) and _____ (insert the behavior from column 4 and corresponding "ish"). I do this because....

☼ Look at "How did this affect me?" (column 3). What needs were affected? Safety? Security (financial or emotional)? Social belonging (personal or intimate)? Esteem? Or Ambitions?

☼ Fill in the blanks: I do this because my _____ (needs) were threatened.

☼ Continue reviewing each row on your Self-Assessment and, following the steps, write your turnaround statements.

See my example for context.

You don't have to do this alone. Visit www.tracydoyle.life if you need help.

Example from my Turnaround

> ### Complete The Turnaround Statement
>
> When I am gripped by <u>never getting the support that I want</u> (loss, less, or never) fear, I'm <u>thoughtless</u> (thoughtless or dishonest) and my thinking is absorbed with <u>self-importance, self-pity, and self-reliance</u> ("ish and/or seeking").
>
> When I'm <u>self-important</u> ("ish" and/or seeking), <u>I don't listen, become dismissive, and</u> <u>try to prove myself</u> (insert the behavior from "What did I do?" (column 4).
>
> Then I <u>think no one understands my needs because I feel self-pity</u> (insert the behavior from column 4 and corresponding "ish) and <u>then get angry and say I'll do it myself and punish with silence because I'm self-reliant</u> (insert the behavior from column 4 and corresponding "ish").
>
> I do this because my <u>emotional security and esteem</u> (needs) were threatened.

Tips:

- ☼ Take your time with each statement and reflect on what you were afraid of. Add that detail into your statement using the fear reflection below.

- ☼ **Reflection on fear.** Loss: What were you afraid to lose? Less: What were you afraid that you would be less than or get less of? Never: What did you want that you were afraid that you would never get?

You don't have to do this alone. Visit www.tracydoyle.life if you need help.

☼ When you fill in the blanks related to your "ishes" and "acts," be sure to add context if you had thoughtlessness or dishonesty checked off. The reflection questions that follow will guide you on additional behavior you may want to add if they were not listed in your column 4 (What did I do)

☼ **Reflection on thoughtlessness.** Were you disrespectful? Dismissive? Arrogant? Impatient?

☼ **Reflection on dishonesty.** Did you outright lie or lie by omission (meaning, if they didn't ask, you didn't say anything?)

☼ Referring to these reflections when completing each Turnaround statement helps to make them more personal and meaningful to you (refer back to my example).

Turnaround statements help you see *your part* in the struggle. Bringing this awareness to the surface empowers you to take ownership and leads to a meaningful change in your relationships.

Now, create a Turnaround Statement for each row on your Self-Assessment using the step-by-step instructions we reviewed above. You may see patterns as you write. That's good!

Pay attention to what you do once a trigger sparks a foundational belief and ignites fear and self-centered thinking. Specifically, what do you do in the presence of fear? Are you primarily thoughtless (fight) or dishonest (flight)? Be sure to examine the cause (threatened needs). The cause is important. Why? Because it helps us remove blame from our vocabulary!

You don't have to do this alone. Visit www.tracydoyle.life if you need help.

When we recognize that the cause is from our stunted needs, we're shifting our thinking away from "them." You know the things we say, "It's their fault" or "They made me." When we shift away from "them," we're free to focus on what in *us* needs to change rather than what in "them" needs to change. And as we change, we can shift the dynamic of every relationship that we touch.

What Did The Turnaround Reveal?

- ☼ Did you see repetitive patterns? What were they?
- ☼ Was seeking or specific "ishes" associated with the same behaviors? What were they?
- ☼ What fear(s) were often associated with certain behavior, seeking and "ishes?"
- ☼ Were you able to connect the cause of your "acts" to the needs (e.g. security) that were stunted by your earlier life experiences? What needs presented the most trouble for you?

If you were able to recognize the repetition in your behavior and embrace that your acts were caused by threats to either your security, social belonging, esteem, or ambitions, I applaud you! You now know it's not "them!"

You're now ready to face some hard truths and see how unresolved resentment affects your relationships at home and at work.

You don't have to do this alone. Visit www.tracydoyle.life if you need help.

Recognize Your Resentment

In this exercise, we're going to find the origin of your triggers. We'll identify unresolved resentments that remain an influence on your thinking and behavior today. We'll look at how unresolved resentments affect your communication and connection with others.

We're going to look for repetitive behavior and the fear, seeking, and "ishes" associated with it. Why? Because this will help you identify the initial beliefs created by your early life experiences. The beliefs that trigger the Reaction Cascade.

The Turnaround					
Recognize Resentment					
Repetitive behavior	Fear	Seeking or "Ishes"	What needs were threatened?	When did it start?	What belief did you internalize?

You don't have to do this alone. Visit www.tracydoyle.life if you need help.

Review "What did I do?" (column 4) on your completed Self-Assessment:

- ☼ Looking at "What did I do?" (column 4), identify what behavior replays repeatedly. Describe it in one sentence, then add it to the first column of the worksheet.
- ☼ Looking at the behavior, what fear was triggered most frequently? Note it in the second column.
- ☼ Reflecting on the repeated behavior, what parts of "self" (e.g., seeking or "ishes") were the most common? Add them to the third column.
- ☼ What needs were threatened most (esteem, emotional security etc.)? Note them.
- ☼ As you examine the repetitive behavior, look for when it first started. Who did it start with and when?
- ☼ Now, reflect on what they did and identify what belief(s) you internalized from this experience (e.g., "Nobody cares," "I'm not supported," "I don't belong," "I'll never be liked," etc.)?
- ☼ Look at each instance of repetitive behavior. Were the beliefs the same each time? If not, what were the other beliefs you recognized?
- ☼ If you identified more than one repetitive behavior pattern, repeat the exercise so you can identify your internalized beliefs shaped by your early life experiences.

See my example and personal reflection for context.

You don't have to do this alone. Visit www.tracydoyle.life if you need help.

Example from my Turnaround

The Turnaround Recognize Resentment					
Repetitive behavior	**Fear**	**Seeking or "Ishes"**	**What needs were threatened?**	**When did it start?**	**What belief did you internalize?**
Punish with silence Abandon relation-ship Say negative things	Never	Self-pity Self-avoidance	Emotional security Personal relations Intimate relations Esteem	Age 8	I don't belong

Personal Reflection: In this example, I recognized that the belief, "I don't belong," which was created by how Nanny treated me when I was eight years old played out across all my personal and professional relationships. I could see what drove me to pull away from my family. How I abandoned my job despite my manager's support when the promotion was blocked. Understand that when I thought people were talking badly about me, I said negative things and perpetuated the problem.

This revelation showed me that my struggles weren't about "them" mistreating me or being out to get me. *It was all within me.* I was *re-*feeling an old wound. My initial belief, "I don't belong" sparked my foundational belief, "I'm not good enough," which ignited my never fear ("I'll never belong") which fueled my "ishes" and fed my acts. I disconnected. Not them.

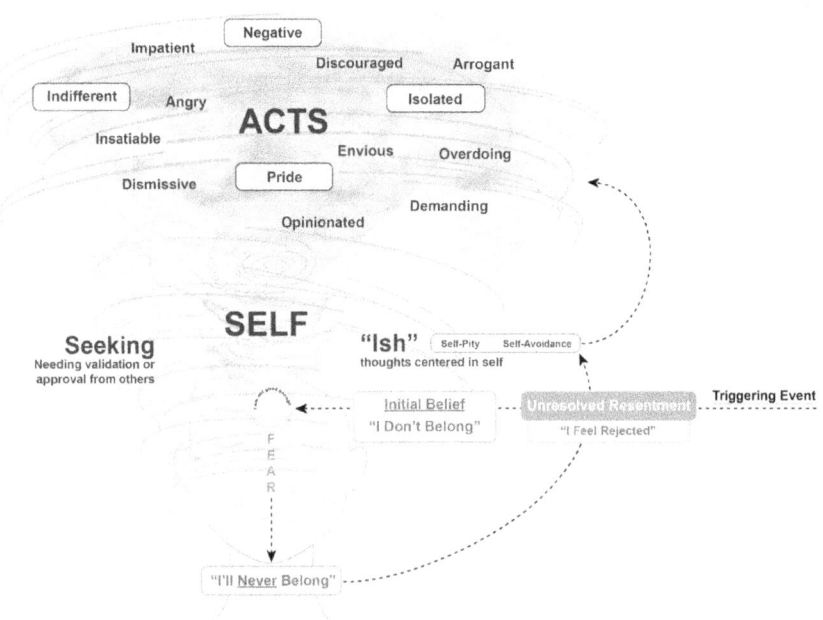

You don't have to do this alone. Visit www.tracydoyle.life if you need help.

This exercise showed me how I internalized my life experiences and how they shaped the following beliefs:

> *I don't belong. I can't trust anyone because they'll hurt me. Nobody cares. Other's needs come before mine. And I must do it all myself.*

These beliefs from my unresolved life experiences wreaked havoc across all my relationships for many years. I struggled with communicating and feeling heard, I struggled with building and maintaining relationships, and I struggled relating to superiors, co-workers, and subordinates. From this exercise, I gained the most profound understanding of all:

Our wounds affect others, too.

You don't have to do this alone. Visit www.tracydoyle.life if you need help.

Recognizing Resentment: A Case Study

To illustrate this exercise further, let's review a case with someone I've coached who agreed to let me share her experience.

She's happily married with children and has a loving husband, beautiful home, a high-powered job, and aging parents. She's everyone's go-to. From the outside, she's seen as the woman who can manage it all. But on the inside, she's struggling. She feels alone, misunderstood, and disconnected from the people she cares about.

Despite being overwhelmed by all the responsibility, she doesn't ask for help. She becomes impatient with her mom. And although she knows her mom has limitations from aging, she gets frustrated and dismissive when her mom doesn't do what she wants her to do about her health. After a bout of impatience, she feels bad about how she acted, feels guilty, then beats herself up.

She also struggles with other family members. When she doesn't feel accepted or supported by them, when she's very overwhelmed, she gets angry, complains, and gossips. When they don't do what she wants them to do, she'll try to force outcomes by demanding or explaining why they need to do what she thinks is right. She feels dejected, sad, or disappointed when her efforts don't yield the results she expected.

When the people in her life pull away emotionally, she becomes needy and wants their approval or validation for feeling the way she does. If she doesn't get the validation she needs, she turns to friends or other family members to reassure her that she's right for feeling the way she does.

You don't have to do this alone. Visit www.tracydoyle.life if you need help.

Now that you understand the Reaction Cascade, let's examine this example:

- ☼ What self-centered thinking (seeking and "ishes?") do you see?
- ☼ We know her "acts" are fed by her thinking. Are her "acts" attracting connection or repelling it? How?

She completed her Self-Assessment and The Turnaround and identified which needs were stunted. She saw how her fear fueled her self-centered thinking patterns. She identified that in the presence of the "Never" fear, her thinking became absorbed with self-importance (she's smarter and knows what's needed), self-righteousness (her way was the only right way), and self-pity (she felt sorry for herself when she believed she would never get the outcomes she wanted). In the face of the "Less" fear, she became self-deprecating (she beat herself up when she thought she was less than who she wanted to be for her family). And in the presence of the "Loss" fear, she became self-seeking (she needed reassurance that the people in her life would not abandon her for her "acts"). This was eye-opening, but the real "AHA" and the motivation to change came when she recognized her resentments.

What was she *re*-feeling? Through the repetitive behavior review, she uncovered the belief, "I'm not accepted," which stemmed from being excluded by a group of girls at school around age ten. She also identified another deeply rooted belief: "I'll never be emotionally supported." A belief that was formed around age twelve, when—feeling insecure about her weight—she sought comfort from a parent but was met with emotional dismissal. These moments, while not traumatic in the traditional sense, left lasting imprints.

You don't have to do this alone. Visit www.tracydoyle.life if you need help.

The way she internalized these experiences shaped beliefs that influenced her behavior, affected her relationships, and undermined her self-worth for years. Through this exercise, she came to see that her present-day relationship struggles weren't about them; they were rooted in the perceived injustices of not being accepted or emotionally supported. She recognized that these unresolved resentments—and the self-centered thinking and acts that followed—were creating emotional distance and unhappiness in her life.

This is the power of unresolved resentment: It doesn't stay in the past. It quietly shapes our present until we have the courage to recognize it, reframe it, and release it.

Now, return to your exercise. What are you *re*-feeling? And what internalized belief is associated to that feeling? How have your beliefs shown up in your relationships? Are they drawing others closer or creating distance?

Unresolved resentment and the initial belief it creates are the triggering events that start every storm.

You don't have to do this alone. Visit www.tracydoyle.life if you need help.

The Reaction Cascade

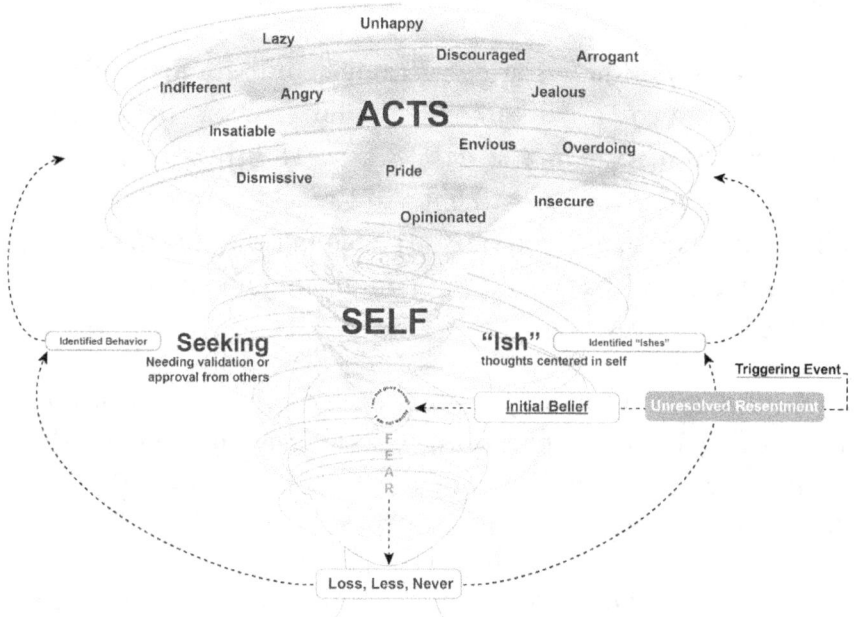

Unresolved resentment resides in the unconscious mind, where past experiences, emotions, and thoughts are stored beyond our conscious awareness. The Aurora Method helps bring these hidden resentments to light, revealing the beliefs, thoughts, and behaviors tied to them, offering hope for change and a path to a better way of being.

Completing The Turnaround is helping you *see*. You've assessed what needs were affected by the experiences in your life. You've identified your primary fears and self-centered thinking patterns and recognized your "acts." You now see how your unresolved resentment has enshrouded you in the "fog" of self-centeredness.

You don't have to do this alone. Visit www.tracydoyle.life if you need help.

You realize that your challenges with the people in your life—spouse, kids, parents, family, friends, and work colleagues—aren't about them but rather are coming from within you.

The key to mindfulness starts with understanding and recognizing that **any time you are disturbed, no matter what someone says or does, *the disturbance is within you*.** The triggering event is our own unresolved resentment. And practicing mindfulness is all about recognizing inner disturbances and addressing them at the source so we have the power to change outcomes with the people in our lives.

Returning to the case study: Once she uncovered what was keeping her stuck and began practicing mindfulness, her relationships with her husband, family, friends, and colleagues started to shift. Not because *they* changed, but because *she* did.

Action *is the solution*. We've got to put this newfound knowledge into practice and learn how to shift our mindset. And once we do, we can find our clear sky.

You've faced hard truths, now give yourself some grace. **Take another break. You've earned it!** And when you're ready, we'll begin building your personalized Life Storm Navigator, a practical tool to help you redirect negative, self-centered thinking and find your clear sky.

You don't have to do this alone. Visit www.tracydoyle.life if you need help.

Finding Your Clear Sky
The Life Storm Navigator

Belonging. We all crave acceptance, whether within our families, friendships, or professional circles. At our core, we long to be part of something greater than ourselves, not because of what we achieve or how we perform, but simply because of who we are. True belonging isn't about doing more, proving ourselves, or meeting expectations. It's about being embraced as we are.

The Self-Assessment and Turnaround help bring clarity. Once we recognize and accept that our thinking contributes to our emotional burnout and relationship struggles, we can act, making real change possible. When I came to this understanding in my own journey, I realized it was time to evolve from a human doing to a human *being*.

I wanted to learn how to be: be okay with who I am, be comfortable among other people, be content with my life, my family, and my career, and—most importantly—be free from the bondage of self-centered thinking, the root cause of my limitations.

Our next quest is learning how to "be."

In *Discover the Power Within You*, Eric Butterworth introduces the concept of "Be Attitudes," or those attitudes we should manifest for abundant living. I was inspired by Butterworth and asked myself, "What attitudes must we change in order to *be*?"

As I reflected on my grandfather's words from years ago, I realized that many of history's greatest teachers—Buddha, Confucius, Jesus, Lao Tzu, Rumi—along with renowned psychologists and self-help pioneers like Wayne Dyer, William James, Susan Jeffers, Carl Jung, Abraham Maslow, and M. Scott Peck share a common foundation for personal growth and transformation.

The principles they taught transcend time, culture, and religious doctrine. They point us toward the same universal truths about the mind, human behavior, and the path to fulfillment. Simply put, mindfulness is putting spiritual practices into action so we can quiet our minds and learn how to "be" in the world.

Their guidance is invaluable, showing us both what to do and what to avoid on our personal development journey. These universal principles form the foundation of the 8 Practices of the Aurora Method: practical, lived experiences that, when followed, lead to real and lasting change.

The 8 Practices: Guiding Principles for Real and Lasting Change

1. The condition or state of our lives is created by our mental attitude; our thinking drives our joy and our hardships.
2. We all can change our thoughts and our beliefs to improve the outer circumstances in our lives, provided we're willing to be open-minded.
3. Seek to understand the truth about yourself to be free from emotional pain and suffering.
4. With an open mind, changing thoughts and beliefs requires letting go of resentment and being ready and willing to adopt new ways of thinking.
5. We must strive to be kind in word, thought, and deed and seek to understand one another before seeking to be understood ourselves.
6. Change in thinking takes time, patience, vigilance, and practice.
7. When the struggles return, re-examine and enhance your daily mindfulness practices.
8. Daily mindfulness practice releases us from fear and the limitations of our thinking.

Through deep self-reflection and commitment to the Self-Assessment and Turnaround process, you're on your way. At this point in the journey, you've been living the first three practices: First, you've accepted your thinking is the problem, then you've opened your mind and become willing to understand how your life experiences have shaped you, and third, you've trusted the process and now understand the truth about yourself.

With this foundation in place, we're now at the fourth practice:

Letting go of old patterns of thinking and adopting new ways of thinking to improve our lives.

Step into Your Personal Transformation

Adopting new ways of thinking requires effort. Shifting away from self-centered thinking isn't just an internal process—it's reflected in our actions. The Turnaround marked the beginning by providing you with self-knowledge. However, simply recognizing your patterns isn't enough. Action, like the athlete seeking to be the best they can be, creates the change needed for true joy and fulfillment.

As we learned earlier, at any point in each day, a triggering event can start the storm. You now know that the triggering event is unresolved resentment, and when you *re*-feel, the storm is swift. Recognizing seeking and "ish" thinking amid daily turbulence, and knowing how to redirect it, is essential for transforming our actions.

When we stay stuck inside the storm, we push others away. When we change our actions, we invite connection and find a true sense of belonging.

You're now at the turning point, the moment in your journey where the rubber meets the road. This is where you're taking what you've uncovered and begin applying it in a way that makes your personal transformation possible. If you're ready to stop letting the scars of unresolved resentment shape your life, it's time to take the steps toward change and reshape it.

Are you ready to step into the life that's waiting for you?

Recognizing self-centered thinking is not intuitive. It takes practice and more practice. What we're about to embark upon is building your own personal tool, The Life Storm Navigator, that will teach you how to shift your mindset. This tool is designed to help you practice changing your thoughts, words, and actions so you can improve your well-being and relationships with others.

Once you create your personal tool, you'll use it in three ways:

- ☼ Practice **recognizing** seeking and "ish" thinking
- ☼ Practice **redirecting** seeking and "ish" thinking
- ☼ Adopt new ways of thinking and being

Let's do this! Your clear sky is waiting above the clouds.

The Life Storm Navigator

The Life Storm Navigator guides you on your mindfulness journey. It will help you elevate self-awareness and practice mindfulness. And it's personal to you because it helps you put into action all that you've learned about yourself through the Self-Assessment and The Turnaround. Since changing thoughts and beliefs can be hard, the Life Storm Navigator becomes your quick reference for use during those inner storms that's often encountered throughout daily life.

How to Get Started:

- ☼ Download and print the Life Storm Navigator at www.tracydoyle.life/Resources. The Worksheet can also be found at the back of this book in the Resources Section.
- ☼ You'll need your completed Self-Assessment and Turnaround. This is a prerequisite. If you skipped ahead, go back and finish up.

There is a new term, "trait," introduced in the Life Storm Navigator. In this context, trait is a universal term referring to self-centered thinking (seeking and "ishes") and the "acts" we wish to change.

What Needs to Change?

To build your Life Storm Navigator, you first need to ask yourself "What needs to change?" Follow the steps below to build your Life Storm Navigator:

- ☼ Refer to "My Fear Patterns," "My Thinking Patterns," and "My Behavior Patterns" on the Turnaround.
- ☼ In the "Trait" column, note the common behaviors in the presence of fear (e.g., dishonesty, thoughtlessness) and the "ishes" identified (include self-seeking if it's one of your patterns). See example for context.
- ☼ Reflecting on the "acts" or the behavior patterns you identified, what behaviors do you want to change (e.g., anger, dismissiveness, jealousy, etc.)? Add them.
- ☼ Once you've completed your list of traits, reflect on what the opposite is for each one. Then put the opposite in the "Opposite" column. (For suggestions, refer to the Life

---

You don't have to do this alone. Visit www.tracydoyle.life if you need help.

Storm Navigator Guide at the back of the book or use Google.)

Example

What Needs to Change? Trait	How Do I Change Opposite
Self-condemnation	Self-praise, nourish, Self-care
Self-importance	Humble restraint
Self-righteousness	Seeking to understand others (beliefs, feelings) first
Thoughtlessness	Think of others
Anger	Calm
Jealousy	Gratitude
Procrastinate	Action

Recognize Seeking and "Ishes"

Learning new ways of thinking that have the power to change our thoughts and beliefs is a process. Why? Because we must bring into conscious awareness what needs to be changed, then reprogram our mind to think and act differently.

Through The Turnaround, you've consciously recognized your patterns. You know it's time to practice change, but you may find that recognizing them during a triggering event isn't so easy. From my own experience, it's much easier to see these traits in others. And I'm sure you'll agree that recognizing shortcomings in others often comes more naturally than acknowledging them in ourselves.

You don't have to do this alone. Visit www.tracydoyle.life if you need help.

The first step in the mindfulness process is recognizing seeking and "ish" thinking. To help you get started, take the "I Spot It" Challenge.

"I Spot It"–14 Day Challenge:

- ☼ This challenge is called "I Spot It!" We're going to practice recognizing seeking, "ishes," and "acts" <u>in others</u>. Refer to your Life Storm Navigator "trait" column then pick three traits that you see in others but may be hard to recognize in yourself.
- ☼ Over the next fourteen days, try to spot your traits in other people.
- ☼ As you spot a trait, note how it affected you. Take a minute and create a voice note:
  - ☼ Name the trait. For example, you might say, *"Today I spotted self-effacing."*
  - ☼ Describe how you felt when you experienced the trait. Here you might say, *"I gave my colleague a compliment about her contributions to our project, and she blushed and said, 'Oh no, it was you who made it great.' I really wanted her to know how much I thought her contributions made a difference and complimented her again. Then she said, 'Oh, it wasn't a big deal. Anyone could have done it.' I felt annoyed and dismissed, I was trying to say something nice and she shut me down.*
- ☼ At the end of each day, review your voice notes and write about what you learned about yourself in relation to each trait. How did it "look?" What was easy for you to recognize in yourself?

You don't have to do this alone. Visit www.tracydoyle.life if you need help.

- ☼ Then think about how you might change it. Referring to our example you might write: *When someone compliments me, even if I'm uncomfortable, I'm going to smile and say thank you.*
- ☼ At the end of week one, pick three more traits and continue the challenge.

Though keep in mind, this challenge is designed to use what we observe in others as *a mirror to identify the same things within ourselves*, not to judge. We are all wounded; we all struggle. This exercise illuminates that. Allow others the grace to find their own path to healing, just as you're doing.

Personal Reflection:
You might not expect to learn much from the "I Spot It" challenge, but you'll be surprised.

In my own journey, I never realized how much validation and approval I was seeking. I thought I was simply asking or checking in to ensure my contributions were recognized. I didn't understand why people became annoyed with me. From the challenge, I saw the frustration and distrust I caused. For example, when I spotted it in subordinates, I found myself getting annoyed that they kept asking me if what they were doing was right. It made me question if I made the right hiring decision. By spotting self-seeking, I learned that refraining from asking might result in harmony rather than distrust or frustration.

An important lesson to remember is that other people's storms can become your triggering events. Think back to the image of how our internal storms can set off reactions in others—this exercise allows you to experience that concept firsthand. The

---

You don't have to do this alone. Visit www.tracydoyle.life if you need help.

more you consciously recognize seeking, "ish" thinking, and the "acts," the better you'll become at identifying them in yourself and knowing how to change them. Once you easily start to recognize your traits, move to the next challenge so you can learn how to redirect them.

Redirect & Manifest

All the great teachers tell us that we can become the change we want to be by manifesting it. But, if you're like me, you don't know how to manifest changes. I found myself printing and hanging sayings or affirmations that resonated with me, but I didn't use them as a part of daily practice. Or more accurately, I would do it for a few days, but when things got better, they just hung on my mirror or cork board until I needed space and discarded them.

Redirecting self-centered thinking requires a daily mindfulness routine. If you don't have a routine, I encourage you to start small and build gradually. Let's pause and review a few simple steps to get you started with mindfulness practice:

Start with just 5 minutes. When you wake up, before picking up the phone or getting out of bed, begin with a short breathing exercise. Take a deep breath, hold it, then count to three, then exhale and count to three. Do this three times. Then…

Practice Gratitude. State two things you're grateful for. For example, "I'm thankful for my health, I'm thankful for my spouse" etc. Then…

You don't have to do this alone. Visit www.tracydoyle.life if you need help.

Read and reflect. Find and read something inspirational, then reflect on what it's trying to teach you. Examples include inspirational readings, devotionals, daily reflections etc.

The key to mindfulness is consistency. Small, mindful moments at the start of each day build a stronger, more intentional mindset over time.

Now, let's get back to how we redirect self-centered thinking and behavior.

The solution for manifesting change is simple: Think and do the opposite.

It may sound easy, but it takes effort. The place to incorporate this practice is in your daily mindfulness routine.

You don't have to do this alone. Visit www.tracydoyle.life if you need help.

"I Am Manifesting"—30-Day Change Challenge

In this challenge, we're going to practice how to redirect seeking, "ish," and acts behavior *before* a triggering event by manifesting change.

- ☼ Refer to your Life Storm Navigator "Trait" and "Opposite" columns.
- ☼ At the end of each day, take ten minutes to reflect about the day. Ask yourself: How did I do today? Did I feel Unheard? Unappreciated? Misunderstood? Frustrated? Angry?
- ☼ If so, reflect on the trigger, then try to identify the "Trait." Remember anytime we're disturbed, the disturbance is within us. We can't blame it on them! We've got to find our disturbance.
- ☼ If you're unable to identify the "trait," look at the "Opposite" column and ask yourself, what do I wish I felt or did instead? Or how would I have wanted to handle that differently?
- ☼ When you find which "Opposite" aligns with what you wanted to feel or do, look at the "Trait" column to identify the trait. Note: There may be more than one.
- ☼ Now, manifest: I am replacing _____ ("trait") with _____ ("opposite"). For example, you may say, *I'm replacing self-avoidance with taking action.*
- ☼ Now, affirm: I am _____ ("opposite"). For example, you may say, *I am taking action*
- ☼ The next morning, after practicing gratitude, affirm what you affirmed the night before.

You don't have to do this alone. Visit www.tracydoyle.life if you need help.

Let me illustrate how. This example is from my Life Storm Navigator.

What Needs to Change?	How Do I Change?
Trait	**Opposite**
Self-avoidance	Take action
Self-importance	Humble restraint
Self-righteousness	Seek to understand others (beliefs, feelings) first
Self-pity	Gratitude
Anger	Calm
Fear	Trust

End-of-day Reflection:

How did I do?	Interactions at work went well, until the call from an angry client. Team was behind in meeting the client's deadline. I reacted and was dismissive during the team meeting.
Trait	Loss fear, self-importance, anger, thoughtlessness.
Manifest	I am replacing fear with trust. I am replacing self-imporatance with kindness, I am replacing anger with calm. I am replacing thoughtlessness with thoughtfulness.
Affirm	I am trusting. I am kind. I am calm. I am thoughtful.

You don't have to do this alone. Visit www.tracydoyle.life if you need help.

Morning Intention:

Take five minutes for mindfulness. When you complete your gratitude practice, affirm the opposites. I'll illustrate this for you by sharing how I practice. It's important to note that this is where I am today after years of practice. All the great teachers suggest aligning your thoughts to a Higher Power or your Higher Self as part of mindfulness practice. When I first started, my practice was simple and followed the format I've outlined. But overtime, my practice has evolved, and today I refer to my Higher Power as God. As you will note below, at times, I speak in the first person while I speak to God.

When I arise in the morning, I take three deep breaths, then I align and speak to God, practice gratitude, and affirm.

> *Your light surrounds me, your love enfolds me, your power protects me, wherever I am, you are. God of my life, I welcome this new day. It is your gift to me. The first day of the rest of my life. Thank you for the gift of being alive this morning. Thank you for the sleep which has refreshed me. Thank you for my spouse's health, longevity, and safety. Thank you for my family's health, longevity, and safety. Thank you for my health, longevity, and safety. We are disease free, and we are worthy of your life and breath. Thank you for one more day of abundant living. I'm impeccable today in word, I'm impeccable today in thought, and I'm impeccable today in deed. <u>I am trusting and I am calm</u>. During this day, <u>I am a more thoughtful person, a kind person, and a more understanding person</u>. I'm alert to my own faults, not to the faults of others. I'm teachable, and I'm focused not on who's right but what's right.*

You don't have to do this alone. Visit www.tracydoyle.life if you need help.

As you can see, I practice what I learned from the Four Agreements by affirming being impeccable in word, thought, and deed. I follow those affirmations by declaring what else I want to manifest throughout the day.

Create and save a Trait and Opposites chart on your phone. While you practice manifesting change during the 30-day challenge, you may encounter daily turbulence. A trigger during a meeting, a trigger while visiting family, etc. Go beyond the morning practice and challenge yourself further.

Quickly refer to your trait and opposites chart on your phone. Then practice the one-minute meditation.

One-minute meditation: During a struggle, disengage (e.g. take a bio break, leave the room, etc.), close your eyes, take a deep breath, and while breathing in, say "I'm breathing in calm" and while exhaling say, "I'm breathing out frustration". Then say, "I am replacing _____ (trait) with _____("opposite")". Then affirm, "I am _____("opposite")".

Now, what about our behavior?" How do we begin to change it? Let's turn back to our Life Storm Navigator to find out how.

You don't have to do this alone. Visit www.tracydoyle.life if you need help.

Complete Your Life Storm Navigator

☼ Go back to your Life Storm Navigator and your completed Self-Assessment to finish the remaining sections.

☼ Start with the third column titled "Trait Behavior."

☼ Review "What did I do?" (column 4) of your Self-Assessment and identify the behavior and/or negative self-talk that corresponds to each trait listed in column 1 of your Life Storm Navigator titled "Trait."

☼ Write your behavior in column three.

☼ Reflect on your trait behavior and write down how you would like to change it in the fourth column titled "Opposite"

☼ Look at your opposites (trait and trait behavior) and reflect on the new thoughts you want to manifest.

☼ Write your personal affirmation in column 5 by thinking about what you want to declare to overcome your trait and trait behavior. Use your opposites as a guide.

See the example for context.

You don't have to do this alone. Visit www.tracydoyle.life if you need help.

Example

LIFE STORM NAVIGATOR				
What Needs to Change?	How Do I Change?	What Needs to Change?	How Do I Change?	Manifest Change New Thought
Trait	Opposite	Trait Behavior /thought	Opposite	Affirm
Self-condemnation	Praise	Blame myself when people are unhappy, feel guilt, "I haven't done enough."	Praise my efforts.	I am enough. I am satisfied with my efforts.
Self-importance	Restraint	Act superior or entitled, criticize.	Remain quiet, listen, acknowledge.	I am kind. I am considerate. I am acknowledging.
Self-righteousness	Understanding	Disagree, argue, criticize, "I'm right."	Listen, seek to understand another's perspective.	I am open and receptive. I am understanding. I am teachable.
Thoughtlessness	Thoughtfulness	Dismissive, interrupt, talk over others.	Pause. Listen. Consider another's feelings and thoughts before speaking.	I am still. I am kind. I am considerate. I am approachable.
Anger	Calm	Criticize, say inappropriate things, yell.	Pause. Breathe. Restraint.	I am centered. I am calm. I am kind.

You don't have to do this alone. Visit www.tracydoyle.life if you need help.

The Life Storm Navigator is your personal tool containing only your traits and opposites. You're empowered to let go of old resentments by manifesting change and connection. But it takes practice, and lots of it. You've begun that practice by reviewing your day and affirming your intentions each morning. Let's harness the winds of change in our daily lives and put the Life Storm Navigator to work so that you can become the change you want to be.

You don't have to do this alone. Visit www.tracydoyle.life if you need help.

Harnessing the Winds of Change
The Connection Builder

Acceptance. The conscious choice to acknowledge something or someone, recognizing what can't be changed while focusing on what can. It serves as the bridge between awareness and healing, helping you to release resistance and begin the process of improving your relationship with yourself and others.

The first part of the Aurora Method Practice 5 embodies acceptance:

We must strive to be kind in word, thought, and deed and seek to understand one another before seeking to be understood ourselves.

Acceptance allows for emotional healing by fostering peace, compassion, and the ability to move forward with clarity and resilience. Through the four practices of the Aurora Method, you've begun to shift your mindset and transcend self-centered thinking. You're accepting how you create struggles, and you've recognized that you can lead the journey of healing and connection in your relationships. Acceptance shifts our mindset from dwelling on the past to creating a more fulfilling future.

The Aurora Method is opening the door to change and empowering you to grow. But I must warn, beware of resistance!

Prior to doing the Self-Assessment and Turnaround, I'd regarded myself as a kind, understanding, and helpful person. I believed people took me the wrong way and couldn't see my intentions. What *I* couldn't see, however, was how my self-centered thinking and "acts" affected others. I was anything but kind and understanding. I may have been helpful, but the wrath people had to endure, at times, while receiving my help made it difficult for them to receive.

My view of the world through fogged lenses created my struggles, created my pain, and put distance between me and those I wanted in my life. The fog isolated me. I was alone with my self-centered thinking, which perpetuated my feelings of separateness. But once my unresolved resentments and the havoc they'd wreaked were brought to my conscious awareness, I could *see*.

I was at the crossroads. I needed to decide to change and be willing to do what was necessary. Was I willing? Could I do it? Of course I could.

Then "Never" fear set in.

Where do I start? How do I begin? What do I do? I don't know how! I was gripped by the limited belief that I'll never belong, followed by the belief that I can't trust anyone. These beliefs triggered the two core limiting beliefs that I wasn't good enough and not worthy of people's acceptance. Fear stepped right into the driver's seat and around the racetrack I went.

Nobody likes me anyway, so why bother (at work)? *My mother and sister are mentally ill. They're not capable of understanding me, so what's the point? My aunt and uncle? Their lives are abundant with their children and grandchildren. They don't have time. And people at work? No! I can't be vulnerable at work. What are my friends going to think? Is all this worth the effort? I can't trust anyone! Well, you can trust your life partner, so that's one person, at least.*

Are you as exhausted reading this as I was thinking it? Resistance to change—it's powerful. And our struggle begins inside, fighting the strong waves of doubt trying to overtake us.

I had what I needed to change right in front of me. Fear was limiting me *again!* I understood the part my thinking played in my sense of responsibility for my mother and my siblings and how my fear of saying no created turmoil in all areas of my life, especially at work. I became angry when people didn't understand what I was asking them to do, a replay of not being understood by my mom.

I learned how self-seeking affected my relationships at home and created distrust with work colleagues. I saw how my "Never" and "Loss" fears fueled my inconsiderate behavior. The street-girl fighter came out to protect me, unmindful that the fight was no longer necessary in a professional setting. I was self-important, and I needed to be right all the time, especially when I didn't feel understood. My pride had held me back from mending relationships with people that mattered most in my life.

There were many things I had to change if I wanted to feel accepted and belong, but figuring out where to start and with who felt paralyzing.

But whenever I'm overwhelmed, I go back to something I learned at a personal growth workshop while in college. At the closing session, the workshop leader talked about the importance of prioritizing what we'd learned so that we could put it into practice. He said, "Just remember, if you see the watermelon on the road, slice it."

He went on to explain that when we learn new things about ourselves, we can't—like a watermelon—take it all in at once. He said, "You can't eat the entire watermelon and swallow it whole, can you? No, you slice it, remove the rind, cut it into small chunks, remove the seeds, then eat it piece by piece."

Changing into who we want to become is the watermelon. We must recognize and embrace the opportunity to change one thing and one person at a time. So, as I say to myself often, I say to you now: *Slice the watermelon.*

I'm guessing you may have had a similar experience when you completed and reviewed your Turnaround and Life Storm Navigator. Specifically, that you came to the realization that you were living life in a state of discontentment and coming from a place of lack or looking at life through a straw.

When you look through a straw, your vision is limited. When living in discontentment and lack, your only focus is on what you don't have, rather than what you do have. And when someone does or says something to reinforce an old belief, we say *"See?"* In my case it was, *"See?* Nobody cares. *See?* You can't trust people because they'll hurt you. *See?* You'll never belong."

As we learned from Maslow, the feelings of discontentment and lack come from our life experiences stunting our growth. We become fearful and self-centered. As wounded people, we're blindly walking through life, *re*-feeling our wounds, acting on them, and remaining stuck inside the fog. We're in a city of limitations unable to get out because we're holding ourselves back and thinking it was everyone else who created those limits.

But now you're able to free yourself from these limitations because you've brought into your conscious awareness fears, self-centered thinking, and the behaviors that create your struggles. You know what the problems are that need to be changed. You've been practicing manifesting change to redirect those old negative thoughts with new, positive ones.

With the foundation you've built through manifesting, we can now focus on what you're going to change, with who, and how you're going to do it. We're going to slice the watermelon, and we'll no longer focus on "them" and what they've done. We're going to focus on identifying the inner disturbance and redirecting it so you can heal and grow with each person that you want to improve your relationships with.

So how do we begin?

We start with acceptance. Accepting that we can't change what happened to shape our beliefs, but with courage, we can change and reshape them now.

If we want a full and abundant life, we must practice changing our thinking. The healing process starts from the inside. We must first look at ourselves with kindness and understanding like we would a friend. You've been through a lot and didn't know how to be. Give yourself a loving hug.

Let's walk through a kind and loving look-back. Read aloud if you feel comfortable:

> *I was wounded. And how I internalized my wounds shaped my core beliefs. I thought I wasn't good enough and I wasn't worthy. But now I know that when I re-feel my wounds, those beliefs get triggered, ignite my fear, and manifest as self-centered thoughts and behavior.*

Now, raise your arms to the sky and say:

> *I'm free from self-centeredness. I'm overcoming my limiting beliefs. I'm kind. I'm thoughtful. And I'm opening my heart and mind to receiving love and healing. I'm loved, and I'm forgiving.*

Now, praise yourself:

> *I'm proud of my commitment to growth and the effort I've put into becoming more self-aware and intentional. I'm embracing challenges as opportunities. I'm resilient. I'm becoming the best version of me.*

The first thing I had to change was recognizing the abundance in my life. I had to put down the straw I was viewing the world through. Through the straw, I didn't have a mother or siblings I could have a give-and-take relationship with. I felt alone because I was the caretaker and the doer for them; I felt like Cinderella. I gave, and I gave. I did, and I did. And I received nothing in return except perpetual betrayal and more demands. I was living in a place of discontentment and lack.

But after I put the straw down, I saw that—yes—I was the caretaker, but I wasn't alone. I was surrounded by a beautiful partner who loved, nurtured, and took care of me. A mother- and father-in-law who were loving, caring, and guiding me. Aunts and uncles who were proud of me. Incredibly kind, loving, and understanding friends who walked through life and its storms with me. I was blessed with an amazing job and surrounded by many talented people who wanted the same outcome as me. Without the straw, I was looking at a big, bright, abundant blue sky.

I'd like you to put down your straw. Describe what you see.

Next, we have to improve how we feel about ourselves. In the book, *52 Weeks of Esteemable Acts: A Guide to Right Living*, Francis Ward teaches us that self-esteem comes from doing esteemable things. Self-esteem comes from behaving in a way that makes you feel good about yourself, which means being mindful of how you treat yourself and how you treat others.

Who do you want to improve your relations with? Yourself? Others? Which relationships matter most to you? Or, said another way, which relationships would you like to strengthen or heal? Let's work together to restore connection in your life.

The Connection Builder

The purpose of the Connection Builder is to show you how to improve your relationships. This is the tool that brings all your work to life. The Connection Builder is the difference maker because it provides practical action steps that you can use daily.

How to Get Started

- ☼ Download and print the Connection Builder at www.tracydoyle.life/Resources. The Worksheet can also be found at the back of this book in the Resources Section.
- ☼ You'll need your completed Self-Assessment and Life Storm Navigator. This is a prerequisite. If you skipped ahead, go back and finish up.

Who Do I Need to Repair Relationships With?

- ☼ Refer to your completed Self-Assessment.
- ☼ Review "What Did I Do?" (column 4) and ask yourself: was there anything I did in response to column 2 that was hurtful, unkind, or thoughtless to the person in column 1? If yes, who was it that you hurt?
- ☼ Write the person's name in column 1 of the Connection Builder titled "Who" (it's okay if you write your own name). If you're struggling to identify who you may have hurt, refer to the "trait behaviors" listed on your Life Storm Navigator. Ask yourself who does or who did these behaviors affect? If someone comes to mind, add them to the "Who" column.

You don't have to do this alone. Visit www.tracydoyle.life if you need help.

☼ Reflect and ask yourself: What did I do that was hurtful or unkind? Write it down in the second column titled "How Was I Hurtful or Unkind?"

You may question the hurt because it's likely something that happened years ago. Remember, your unresolved resentment patterns from The Turnaround! And the seeking, "ishes" and acts that follow. Look to them to help you identify a possible hurt.

☼ Now, think about what esteemable act you can do for the person listed in column 1.

To help you get started, refer to your Life Storm Navigator and look to the fourth column titled "How Do I Change?" Look at the Opposite you listed.

☼ Reflect on the Opposite, then write down what you can and will strive to do in column 3 of the Connection Builder titled "What esteemable act can I do?"

☼ Finally, in the last column, write down how you'll do it. Refer back to your Life Storm Navigator. Look at the new thought or affirmation you identified. Remember the affirmation pertains to your trait. Reflect and write down what you'll affirm related to your dealings with the person listed on your Connection Builder.

See my example for context.

You don't have to do this alone. Visit www.tracydoyle.life if you need help.

Example from my Connection Builder

Connection Builder			
Who	**How was I hurtful or unkind?**	**What esteemable act can I do?**	**How will I do this?**
Mom	I yell when she doesn't understand me. I disappear for days, weeks, or months.	Stay calm, do my best to understand, listen, and remain in her life.	I'll silently affirm that I'm calm and understanding.
Mom	I get dismissive when she calls me at work because she doesn't understand my job demands.	Set boundaries by calmly saying I'm happy to help at X time.	I'll silently affirm that I'm safe, and it's okay to say no.
Co-workers	I become impatient, interrupt, and dismissive when pressured for time.	Breathe, communicate availability, do a time check and schedule more time if needed.	I'll silently affirm that I'm centered, calm, open and receptive.
Life Partner	I repeatedly ask if she loves me	Refrain	I'll silently affirm, that I'm secure and loved.
Life Partner	Give silent treatment and get short when she doesn't acknowledge me when I get home from work	Communicate my desire to talk when she's ready.	I'll silently affirm that I'm secure and loved.

You don't have to do this alone. Visit www.tracydoyle.life if you need help.

The Connection Builder Is Essential for Your Transformation

The Connection Builder provides a clear, actionable plan for practicing change in your relationships. When frustration, misunderstanding, or anger arise, you'll have a practical approach to shift your thoughts and actions toward connection. While change takes time, this tool helps you pause, redirect negative thinking, and respond more intentionally, preventing conflict from lingering. With practice, it can truly change the course of your life.

Prioritize

When you're done, you'll have a list of the people in your life who you can improve or restore connection with. Let's not forget the watermelon. We can't change everything with everyone at once. We must slice the watermelon and eat it piece by piece. This means we need to prioritize who on our list we want to start practicing change with.

Refer to page two of the Connection Builder titled "Connection Priorities" and using the Reflection Questions provided, prioritize your list into three categories: Immediate, Later, and Never.

You don't have to do this alone. Visit www.tracydoyle.life if you need help.

Reflection Questions

- ☼ Who in your life are you ready to improve relationships with now? Note their names in the Immediate column.
- ☼ Who is important to you but you're not quite ready to improve your relationship with them in the near term? Note their names in the Later column.
- ☼ Who in your life have you chosen not to re-engage with for your well-being and growth? Write their name in the Never column. These are typically people who are no longer a part of your life for clear and significant reasons, such as past trauma, abuse, or other harmful experiences.
- ☼ Who in your life do you wish you could have improved relationships with before they passed away? How would you prioritize them if they were here? Add their names to the appropriate column.

Example from my Connection Priorities

Connection Priorities		
Immediate	**Later**	**Never**
Life Partner	Aunt Ann	Uncle
Mom	Uncle Tim	
Mam	Sister	
Me	Subordinate A	

Once your list is prioritized, you're ready to begin the healing process! The priority list is your roadmap, and your Connection Builder and Life Storm Navigator together are your compass.

You don't have to do this alone. Visit www.tracydoyle.life if you need help.

These tools give you guidance and direction on how to practice change from this point forward.

Before we move on, let's ground ourselves on what we've learned so far about restoring connections and practicing change.

As you continue moving toward personal growth and connection, keep these lessons in mind:

- ☼ **Slice the watermelon:** Digest what you've learned and then focus.
- ☼ **Accept the past, shape the future:** You can't change what's behind you, but you now have the tools to change what's ahead.
- ☼ **Do the kind and loving look-back:** Make this affirmation a habit to support progress and growth.
- ☼ **See the positives:** Put your straw down and see beyond it, daily.
- ☼ **Prioritize:** Create your Connection Builder, then prioritize who matters.

"The greatest gift you
can give someone
is acknowledgement."

—Oprah Winfrey

Clearing the Skies
Emotional Healing Begins with Acknowledgement

Understanding. The ability to listen and see situations from another person's perspective without judgment or defensiveness. Recognizing another's emotions, needs, and experiences as valid, even if they differ from your own.

The second part of Practice 5 embodies understanding:

We must strive to be kind in word, thought, and deed and **seek to understand another before seeking to be understood ourselves.**

I had an epiphany about how to strengthen understanding while listening to Oprah Winfrey speak at an event in Newark, New Jersey. Understanding fosters deeper connection, reduces conflict, and creates space for meaningful communication. It's the foundation for trust, compassion, and lasting relationships. Understanding is possible with acknowledgement. I strive to live by it every day.

Mending Relationships Starts with Acknowledgement

From the Connection Builder, we see what relationships we need to repair and how to do it. To jump-start connection, initiating a conversation that fosters understanding can build a bridge between you and the other person.

Once you've decided who you want to improve connection with first, begin practicing change by going beyond a mere apology and start with acknowledgement. Saying "I'm sorry" often perpetuates resentment in those we've hurt. Why? Because when we do or say something hurtful, our default is to say, "I'm sorry" and move on, expecting them to get over it, only to repeat the behavior again at another time. **We don't change**.

How many times are you going to say, "I'm sorry?" Make the decision to move beyond that and embrace acknowledgement.

Acknowledgment provides an opening. It gives us an opportunity to start a dialogue with someone we're trying to improve relations with. It makes room for them in our lives because it opens the door for change. Acknowledgement fosters understanding.

I must point out, however, that acknowledgement isn't about explaining yourself. How many times have you tried to have a conversation with someone with the intent of improving the relationship, only to find yourself deeper in the struggle— misunderstood, frustrated, and, ultimately, ready to give up?

I've reflected on this challenge countless times, both in my own life and in my work with others. One of the most powerful insights I've learned is the importance of avoiding **JADE**.

When we JADE, we do the following:

- ☼ **J**ustify our behavior or critical words, ignoring the harm we've done and leaving the other feeling unheard and misunderstood.
- ☼ **A**rgue why we're right for doing or believing what we do without taking the time to understand. There's only one winner, leaving the other feeling unheard and dejected.
- ☼ **D**efend our behavior by dismissing another's feelings and fail to recognize harm done, leaving others hurt and misunderstood.
- ☼ **E**xplain why our behavior is the way it is because of what the other person did, leaving no room for mutual understanding and alienating the person.

JADE hurts. It keeps us tucked inside the safety and comfort of our self-centered thinking, perpetuating old beliefs and negative thinking. There's no understanding when we approach a conversation with JADE. When we feel unheard or misunderstood, it's easy to fall into one of the JADE traps, desperately trying to make someone else understand. But instead of fostering connection, **JADE fuels conflict**, reinforcing the very struggles we're trying to resolve. We then fall into the belief that no matter what we do, things will never get better, so we quit and stay stuck.

Let's break that cycle.

You don't have to do this alone. Visit www.tracydoyle.life if you need help.

JADE provides guidance on what to avoid when practicing acknowledgement with someone you'd like to improve your relationship with.

Remember JADE when you're interrupted, and you find yourself justifying or arguing your point.

Remember JADE when you encounter tit for tat, and you become defensive.

Remember JADE when you find yourself getting caught up in the "why" you did something.

Refrain from JADE and focus only on how your actions may have hurt the person and acknowledge it. Use your affirmations to stay centered and have a calm conversation.

This simple shift transformed my conversations, helping me approach difficult discussions with a sense of calm and confidence. The moment I stopped engaging in JADE, I saw a real change in how I communicated and how others responded.

Strive to master this, and you'll reap the benefit of emotional healing and true connection.

You don't have to do this alone. Visit www.tracydoyle.life if you need help.

Navigating the Acknowledgement Conversation

There are many ways to acknowledge. Let's explore them using examples from my journey.

Refrain to Acknowledge: It Builds Esteem

After completing my Connection Builder, my immediate priority was my partner. I frustrated her by constantly asking her if she loved me. And when she didn't say "I love you" unprompted, I would say, "Nobody cares," and she would—understandably—get angry. I also wanted her to validate me by giving me a hug and asking about my day when I got home from work. When she didn't, I gave her the silent treatment because I thought I wasn't asking for much. But as I looked at the Self-Assessment and went deeper with my Turnaround, I saw that I wasn't considering her feelings in my quest for attention.

With that insight, the first change was to refrain from asking. The cause, after all, was driven by my stunted emotional security, so nothing she could say or do could fix those feelings inside me. I practiced refraining by using the plan and personal affirmations I created in my Life Storm Navigator and Connection Builder.

In this example, I made the change without the acknowledgement conversation. The only conversation necessary was the silent one with myself to combat my fear. This is a great way to get started. Look at your Connection Builder and Connection Priorities, identify what you can change without the conversation and practice change using your personal affirmation(s). You'll be glad you did.

You don't have to do this alone. Visit www.tracydoyle.life if you need help.

Refraining from self-seeking behavior improved our relationship almost immediately. And over time, as I continued to practice, my partner validated me unprompted.

Practicing refraining helped me go beyond my partner. When I realized how self-seeking affected all my relationships, I stopped asking, and I gave people a chance to acknowledge me. Refraining enriched my relationships at home, with family and friends, and at work. The more I practiced refraining, the more secure I became with myself. This esteemable act truly improved my esteem!

Kindly Acknowledge: It Brings Harmony

The second change with my partner was related to my expectations. In his book *The Truth: An Uncomfortable Book About Relationships*, Neil Strauss introduced the idea that when we remain silent about our expectations, they are really premeditated resentments. I would argue that they're not premediated. Rather, they're unresolved resentments. Nevertheless, Neil Strauss's writing helped me realize my expectation was for my partner to know what I needed without me telling her. And when she didn't give me what I expected, I perpetuated the unresolved resentment I had with my mom. I was treating my partner like I had my mother many years ago. I would punish with silence and distance. These behaviors caused problems because they became her triggering event. All I wanted was closeness, but while living life in the fog of self-centeredness, I created anything but. I realized how I needed to change and put that into practice immediately after I acknowledged the problem I was creating in our relationship.

My acknowledgement conversation sounded like this: "I've been reflecting lately about our relationship and realized how unfair I've been. I haven't told you how important it is to me to hug and talk to you when I get home from work. Instead, I've been quietly expecting you to do it, and when you don't, I get pouty and give you the silent treatment. And when you're ready to talk and engage with me, I'm distant, say unkind things, and get short with you. But I'm not going to do that anymore because it's hurtful to you and to us."

The look on my partner's face was surprise, then relief. She thanked me for recognizing the problem and reminded me that she loved me very much, but when I got like that, she didn't know what to do. Well, how could she have? I didn't tell her!

My actions through the acknowledgement conversation brought us together and created harmony, and I've since continued practicing acknowledgement with her across many things that come up. And the result is consistent: understanding and loving kindness.

Written Acknowledgement: It Paves the Way to Self-forgiveness

How do you repair a relationship with someone who's no longer with us? One of my greatest regrets was not being there for my grandmother in the last few years of her life. Although Mam wasn't on my Self-Assessment, I was. I was angry with myself. I was guilt-ridden. She'd done so much for me and my family, and I didn't give back. She was an immediate on my priority list, but the mending that was needed wasn't with her—it was with myself.

I decided to write her a letter. I found healing in acknowledging my regret and expressing my gratitude. I had the opportunity to tell her how unthinking I'd been and thank her for her commitment and love to our family. All she ever wanted was for me to do well, to see the world, and help our family in a time of need. I promised her that I would. And I've kept that promise.

Show Up to Acknowledge: It Restores Connection

My relationship with my Aunt Ann and Uncle Tim meant the world to me. But after our falling out, two deep resentments reinforced my old beliefs: don't trust anyone because they'll hurt you and I don't belong. I stayed distant for over ten years. Despite their efforts to reconnect and my own desire for closeness, "Never" fear and self-avoidance held me back. I labeled them as "Later" on my Connection Priorities, avoiding the emotional waves of my resistance.

Eventually, I realized I had to break through my resistance and face it if I wanted to repair our relationship. I began redirecting my thinking: *I'm removing fear and replacing it with trust. I'm removing self-pity and replacing it with gratitude.* I thanked God for their role in my life and affirmed: *I'm open and receptive to a conversation. I'm trusting that all will go well. I'm loved.*

This practice manifested an unexpected call—my aunt had been diagnosed with breast cancer. In that moment, I let go of fear and showed up. And when I arrived, she was emotional and deeply relieved. That single act of presence began the healing.

I listened to and supported her. We spoke often and processed the diagnosis and all the fear it brought. I gave her Louise Hay's book, *You Can Heal Your Life.*

I sat quietly with my uncle, a man of few words, who was devastated at the thought of losing the love of his life.

I walked through the journey with them.

Manifesting and affirming helped me recognize the opportunity to heal and mend two of the most meaningful relationships in my life. Showing up is a powerful act of love. It acknowledges, even without words, that you care. It says, you matter. And often, that single step opens the door to a deeper acknowledgment conversation when the heart is ready.

Prepare, Then Acknowledge: It Fosters Healing

Now, let's explore a hard conversation: My mother.

My mom's poor choices, physical and emotional abuse, and inability to nourish and guide me were *deep* wounds. How could I forgive and, more importantly, acknowledge and open the door? I spent much of my life explaining and justifying my behavior by making it about her. She did this, and naturally I did that. If she hadn't done this, I wouldn't have acted that way. But as we've learned, there's no emotional accountability in that type of thinking and behavior, and it's certainly not going to foster personal growth and connection. Instead, it'll perpetuate the problem.

Therefore, committed to embracing a new solution, I embarked on a deep reflection. This introspective journey led me to a profound understanding. My experiences with my mom were related to the fact that there was no diagnosis at that time; her bipolar disorder was never treated. She had no help with her mental illness and, in the absence of insight, she didn't have the ability to recognize and learn from her wrongs.

I struggled with this conversation because, at times, I felt deep resentment toward her. The constant stress of dealing with her financial irresponsibility, her lack of awareness about my career demands, and her overall inability to manage her life left me conflicted. And when I tried to set boundaries, she lashed out, calling me a selfish bitch, or turned vindictive by reaching out to people I cared about to turn them against me. The betrayal cut deep, leaving me torn between protecting myself and repairing our relationship. Was it worth it?

Managing my mother took its toll on me financially and emotionally. When I felt unappreciated or misunderstood at home or at work, those triggering events led to volcanic eruptions, and at times rageful outbursts. My only way to cope with my mother was to punish her by abandoning her, ignoring her calls, and refusing to handle her problems.

The Self-Assessment and Turnaround revealed my unkindness. I didn't accept her mental illness, craving understanding she couldn't give. Managing her condition created a belief that others' needs always came before mine, and in the process, I lost myself. The solution was putting my needs first and asserting myself calmly with her, but the thought terrified me. I felt paralyzed thinking about it. I didn't want to deal with her yelling and the insults that would follow.

I recognized that having a mom with mental illness meant I had to go beyond the straw. She longed for closeness and love but was only capable of having a one-way relationship. She wanted to be heard, be praised, and treated with kindness, understanding, and compassion, but she didn't have the ability to reciprocate consistently. Moreover, her constant betrayals were a part of her mental illness, not inherently *her*. If I wanted to improve my relationship with her, I had to come to a place of acceptance, which meant abandoning the idea that she could or would reciprocate and forgive her betrayal. I had to be willing to accept whatever it was that she could give.

The opportunity to open the door started with acknowledgement, but it took courage. I had to admit to myself that abandoning her had been unkind and likely caused her to live in distress and fear. My responses had caused her harm too, and to find forgiveness in my heart, I needed to change.

JADE mattered here. I couldn't justify, argue, defend, or explain. I had to prepare to overcome it and redirect myself to calm because whenever I tried to talk to my mother calmly and rationally, she would interrupt and turn the conversation into something entirely different, and I would either erupt or shut down. During the eruptions, I would ragefully justify, argue, or defend. During the shutdowns, I would try to explain myself to be understood, then withdraw. But no matter what I did, the exchange would devolve to misunderstanding and more anger on both sides. No connection was possible that way.

I needed to mentally prepare and envision this conversation. When I finally had the courage, this is how I approached the conversation: "Mom, I've been reflecting a lot lately about our relationship, and I realized that when I try to talk to you about something, and you get frustrated with me, I—"

She reacted, interrupted me, and started yelling. But I was prepared. I silently affirmed, "I am calm" and I remained calm. I waited patiently until she was done raging and calmly said, "Are you done? Please hear me out."

I told her that I realized that when I'd get upset with her, I'd punish her by abandoning her for weeks, months, and years and how unkind and scary that must have been for her. She burst into tears and told me how she felt all those times that I'd abandoned her. I acknowledged her feelings then committed to do my best, to stay in her life from that day forward.

This was the start of our healing journey. I established healthy boundaries, visited or called weekly, and I not only felt good about our relationship, I felt good about myself. I was acting esteemable.

Acknowledgement Builds Connection

The act of acknowledgement helps to build esteem. When you acknowledge, not only does the person you're acknowledging heal, but you heal as well. When you practice acknowledgement, you'll find that each time you mend a relationship with someone, you'll feel good.

The greatest insight I gained from mending through acknowledgement was that it only takes one person in any relationship to lead change—with your spouse or significant other, with members of your family, with friends, with your boss or colleagues at work, or any other relationship that is important to you. All it takes is courage and willingness to lead. Prior to acquiring this belief, I resisted this idea and would ask myself, "Why do I always have to put myself aside and do everything?!"

But leading change has nothing to do with putting yourself aside or losing yourself. It's about improving your esteem and finding and keeping close connections and bringing joy into your life. By understanding how your wounds affected your thinking and actions, you're empowered to free yourself from your struggles.

You don't have to do this alone. Visit www.tracydoyle.life if you need help.

Clearing the skies means mending the relationships that matter to you and restoring connections.

I encourage you to continue this journey and heal through acknowledgment. The rewards are life changing.

Some of us, however, may need professional support with this process. If you're struggling, I urge you to engage a therapist. Share your insights from the Aurora Method to help deepen your progress and prepare for acknowledgment conversations.

Recognizing how wounds shaped my thoughts and actions transformed me. Mending relationships through acknowledgment nourished me. I was filled with positivity, deep gratitude, and profound acceptance and understanding.

By accepting my mother's limitations, I realized everyone has limitations and that none of us truly understands what another person needs. We've all been wounded and use our own framework of experiences to interact in the world. From these experiences, we think people should do this or do that, or we have very strong opinions on *who* is right rather than focusing on *what* is right.

We've learned how internalizing our life experiences differs for each of us. And why our wounds matter—they matter in how we receive and respond to what a person says or does. Most people don't intentionally trigger us. We're the ones "miss taking" them because we are *re*-feeling unresolved resentments and responding in a self-centered way.

When we approach relationships from a place of understanding, we open the door. We keep the door open by avoiding JADE.

You don't have to do this alone. Visit www.tracydoyle.life if you need help.

Recognizing that someone's inner storms might trigger ours means we need to first seek to understand *them*—exploring what they meant by something they said or did and acknowledging it—before trying to be heard or understood ourselves. Acknowledgement conversations lead the way because they embody Practice 5 of the Aurora Method. Acknowledgement helps us to seek to understand first, then strive to be kind in word, thought, and deed.

You're now prepared for maintaining what you've learned through daily practice. But before we move on, let's pause and reflect on all that you've gained:

Our wounds matter. We internalize our life experiences differently, and understanding how they affect us begins the journey of personal growth.

Anytime we are disturbed, the disturbance is within us. Unresolved resentment and the initial belief are the triggering event, igniting fear and fueling self-centered thinking and behavior. Learn to recognize the beliefs causing your inner turbulence.

Adopt new ways of thinking. Redirecting how we respond to the inner turbulence fosters the mindset shift away from self-centeredness and toward others.

Break the cycle of negative thinking. Overcome resistance and commit to daily practice.

Think and do the opposite. Manifest and affirm the change you want to be through mindfulness practice.

You don't have to do this alone. Visit www.tracydoyle.life if you need help.

Acknowledge and mend. Acknowledgement opens the door to healing and connection.

Lasting change is possible. It only takes *one* person to lead it. You are that person. Commit!

> "Life is a journey,
> not a destination."
>
> —Ralph Waldo Emerson

Peering Above the Storm

Comfort Can Lead to Complacency

Contentment. A sense of happiness and satisfaction, independent of external circumstances. We are content when we accept the present moment, appreciate what we have, and let go of the need for constant validation.

The Aurora Method is your guide to connection and personal fulfillment. Its practices are designed to help you cultivate inner peace by navigating internal turbulence, embracing acceptance and understanding, and fostering genuine contentment in your relationships.

At this point in the journey, you've identified your unresolved resentments, the initial beliefs that they created, and the fear and self-centered thinking they trigger. You've been actively shifting your mindset by thinking and doing the opposite, and you've made progress improving your relationships using acknowledgment. Through these practices, you're building your esteem, you're more aware, and your relationships are improving. You feel content.

But...

You find yourself back in the struggle at times, right?

You've experienced feeling good, you've seen what good looks like, then you have a storm "flare." What's this about, you ask? Then you find yourself going back to fear, seeking, "ishes," and "acts." Then you start to think, "Everything's okay. We all make mistakes," or you may go deep into an "ish" and tell yourself you're a failure, that things will *never* change.

Let's start there. Growth isn't about passing or failing. It's about patience. Remember the kind and loving look-back? Progress takes time and practice, yet we often stop when things improve. Why is that?

Deceptive contentment. Deceptive contentment gives the illusion of fulfillment, leading to complacency and the abandonment of the very practices that sustain growth, connection, and well-being. When life improves, it's easy to believe we no longer need to practice, only to face the consequences later. Change requires the willingness to stay aware of self-centered thinking and behavior. Practice 6 of the Aurora Method is pivotal because it tells us that we shouldn't stop and embrace the idea that **change in thinking takes time, patience, vigilance, and practice.**

Patience is essential, as true transformation takes time and consistent effort. The vital skill that Practice 6 encourages is vigilance.

Vigilance Is Essential for Our Continued Growth

Vigilance is the practice of maintaining constant awareness of fear and self-centered thinking to prevent falling into autopilot reactions or "acts." We started practicing vigilance with the end of day reflection during the "I Am Manifesting" challenge. And we started practicing daily vigilance using the one-minute meditation. Vigilance ensures that mindfulness isn't just a passive state but an ongoing, engaged effort to stay present and self-aware.

By staying aware and mindful of our actions and reactions, we can break through negative thinking, make intentional choices, and create lasting change. While this all sounds good, the reality for most of us is that when things begin to improve, we stop our practices.

In the absence of daily practice—I can attest—reactions come back, *often without warning*. Vigilance is crucial in recognizing self-centered thinking because it allows us to catch and redirect seeking and "ish" thoughts before they take root and unconsciously drive the "acts." Conversely, vigilance helps us quickly recognize what happened after we react to a trigger so that we can address, acknowledge, and mend it. In either case, *vigilance matters*.

Storms and inner turbulence persist; we never graduate from life and its storms. Embracing the lessons of Practice 6—time, patience, vigilance, and practice—equips us to navigate the ever-changing skies with awareness and resilience.

After completing the Aurora Method, I focused on improving my personal relationships first.

I practiced and practiced, and when things improved, I stopped. Let's review some of the lessons I learned from abandoning practice, highlighting why Practice 6 is so essential in our personal development journey.

Lesson 1: Making Time Matters.

I'd made great strides in my personal relationships. I practiced refraining, acknowledged and mended, and things were going well; I felt content. During this time, I'd started a new job at a start-up company. Blinded by excitement, I didn't focus on what I'd learned about myself in work relationships. Namely, that when my financial security or esteem were threatened, the "I'm not good enough belief" triggered my "Loss" fear, which fueled self-importance and self-righteousness. I didn't prioritize improving work relationships. Rather, I took my success for granted.

What this senior vice-president projected into the workplace was arrogance with a tone that "you'd better respect and agree with me, because if you don't, I'll pummel you, since I'm always right." As one might imagine, these behaviors didn't foster harmony and connection with my subordinates. Instead, they caused misunderstanding and frustration. *I was their triggering event.*

A different "ish"—self-avoidance—caused even bigger problems. I didn't lean into leading. I stayed in my comfort zone. I'd spend time brainstorming and selling solutions to clients rather than making time for those who'd needed guidance on how to implement them. The truth was I lacked management experience, and I didn't know how to develop departmental procedures, workflows, and build operational infrastructure. And I avoided by distracting myself with sales activities. When things went wrong, I took matters in my own hands or I blamed others—my team's inexperience or human resources for not hiring the right talent. But as we know, my self-centeredness was the real problem.

I didn't make time for practice, and I certainly didn't make personal growth a priority at work. *I was too busy for that.* My lack of daily mindfulness practice resulted in a performance improvement plan and a coach. I struggled to accept the inevitable truth that failure to make time to improve my self-centered behavior would result in further consequences. Within a few months, I was terminated.

Terminated? I'd just signed a million dollars that day. *Don't you know how valuable I am?* The cause was improper client management. *What? My clients love me. They wouldn't give us business otherwise.* I was in shock. I'd never been fired before. And my boss knew I'd just assumed custody of my niece and nephew and bought a new house to support them. How could he do this to me? N*obody cares. They only care about themselves. Besides, you can't trust anyone.*

Observe how the two initial beliefs created by unresolved resentments ("nobody cares," and "you can't trust anyone") started the cascade. I went right to self-pity rather than get honest with myself that it was me who was unwilling to change and prioritize improving work relationships.

As I drove home, I talked out loud. "Wow, I'm free. I've always felt responsible and obligated. I'm free to chart my own course. Well, everyone always said I should start my own business. Okay, I guess it's time." I felt an overwhelming sense of peace and calm at that moment.

But shortly after, I freaked out. *What am I going to do? I don't have enough experience to start a company. What am I thinking? I need a job. Who's going to hire me? I was just fired. We just bought this house. How are we going to pay for it? What about the kids? How are we going to afford them? I should have prioritized change. You're such an idiot! You just blew the most amazing opportunity. You'll never get ahead!*

Let's look at my freak-out and play "I Spot It." What fear and "ishes" do you see?

If you guessed the "Loss" fear, you spotted it. Observe how my "Loss" fear created a city of limitation by fueling my "ishes." Do you see self-doubt (I don't have enough experience/I'm not good enough) and self-deprecation (I'm an idiot)? And the cascade of negative thinking didn't stop there. My mind went to the "Never" fear (you blew it, you'll never…), and next, took me deeper into self-pity.

It didn't stop there.

I called my mentor, Marianne, for validation that I was a victim. I told her what'd happened. She said, "Why don't you just start your own damn company? You'll do well." When I responded saying, "I can't start a company because I don't know what I'm doing," she scoffed. "Nonsense. You're very talented. You'll figure it out. Now go cry your eyes out, and when you wake up on Monday morning, dammit, you're going to start your own company. Got it?!" After hanging up with her, I'd received numerous phone calls with various opportunities and offers. And my fear quelled a little.

Let's continue with "I Spot It." What do you see now?

If you said "self-seeking," good job! You spotted it. I sought validation about being a victim. What I received in return was encouragement, but my "Less" fear fed my belief that I wasn't good enough to start and lead a company. What's important to observe was how the encouragement came from external voices. Not my own.

In the Absence of Mindfulness, Fear Can Limit Us.

Let's examine my fear.

The storyline in my head about starting my own business was centered on my "Less" fear: *You don't have experience; what are you thinking? You're going to fail.* Then the "Loss" fear: *And if you fail, how are we going to be able to afford the extra expense of the kids and mom's condo? If all your savings goes to them, then we'll lose the house. If we lose the house, then she'll leave me. And if she leaves, I'll be alone. If I'm alone, I'll lose everything. I can't do this!*

Fear: False Events Appearing Real.

Fear isn't based on logic. It's in our mind and creates story after story, often leaving us, as Zig Ziglar said, with a choice: **F**orget **E**verything **A**nd **R**un or **F**ace **E**verything **A**nd **R**ise. The first being limiting and the second empowering.

Fear gripped me, and the grip was tight. The only way to loosen it was to think it through. Unpack it line by line. What was the worst possible thing that could happen? I could fail. BUT, as I saw within an hour of being unemployed, I could get a job. I hadn't lost anything. It was all in my mind.

I took some deep breaths and grounded myself. Then, as my friend Missy often says, I asked myself, "Where are your feet?"

On the floor in our house. I was safe. I was secure. And I wasn't alone. We were okay financially. All was well.

Thinking through fear starts with listening to the story in our mind and unpacking it. Then recognizing the false events that lace the stories and redirecting them.

We learned how to redirect by using personal affirmations. To manage my "Less" fear, I turned back to The Life Storm Navigator to look at my opposites, then I affirmed, "I am good enough, I am capable, and I am trusting this opportunity put before me." And I made the choice. I would face everything and rise.

As you saw, after losing my job, self-centered thinking and fear took control and distorted my perspective. Self-centered thinking can make life's challenges and its storms feel personal, keeping us stuck in negative thinking while fear holds us back from seizing opportunities.

In the absence of daily mindfulness practice and vigilance, our fear, seeking, and "ish" thinking causes us to react negatively and makes it hard to experience peace, fulfillment, and meaningful connections. The hard truth is, we create our struggles. And when faced with the consequences of abandoning mindfulness practice, we often **JADE** and collapse into fear.

Does any of this sound familiar?

Justify. "I didn't see the results. It just wasn't working for me." Or "I just couldn't fit one more thing on my calendar." When we justify why we abandon daily practice, what we really mean is that we didn't commit to or embrace the idea that change takes time.

Argue. "Don't you know how busy I am? I have too many daily responsibilities; I have no time." When we argue why we stopped or can't do it, what we're really saying is change and mindfulness are a low priority, because if it were important to us, we'd do it.

Defend. "Are you kidding me? Why am I the one who has to do everything?" Defending our decision to stop is just another "ish." Can you spot it? Self-avoidance is a big one for many of us. We seem to think it will resolve on its own, which is another "ish!" Do you spot it? Self-deception.

Explain. "I didn't think I needed to do it anymore because everything got better." Explaining is another way of describing deceptive contentment.

I'd realized that I'd become complacent. And my deceptive contentment had clear consequences. When faced with the hard truth of my inaction, I fell back on JADE, arguing, "Who has the time?" and explaining, "Things got better, so I didn't need it," rather than admitting that improving my work relationships wasn't a priority. But reflecting on each JADE excuse for neglecting daily practice reveals a common theme: We don't commit to daily mindfulness practice for the long term.

Without a consistent routine, fear can easily take control—you saw the stories I was telling myself. Returning to the Aurora Method allowed me to dissect each line of my fear narrative, reframe it, and ultimately make a decision that changed the course of my life.

Make the time. It's the difference maker in your life.

Lesson 2: Personal Fulfillment Is an Inside Job

True contentment doesn't come from status, success, or approval. It starts within. When we shift our mindset and learn to redirect fear-based thinking, we create lasting peace and fulfillment, no matter what life throws our way. But that journey isn't always easy, especially when external success masks inner struggle.

Starting a company was exhilarating and terrifying. I co-founded a medical communications company with my best friend, Angela, and another partner. Almost immediately, we saw success. We booked business within weeks and became a multimillion-dollar company in our first year. But that growth came with unexpected challenges.

Early on, I wrestled with my title. CEO? I hadn't earned that. I only had a B.A. in psychology and counseling—no MBA, no executive experience. My inner storm of self-doubt and the "I'm not good enough" belief took over. I worried what others would think. So, I settled on "President," a title that felt safer.

Can you spot how my limiting beliefs "ignited my "Less" fear and fed self-doubt, the "ish" holding me back?

Even as the company took off, our biggest problem was profitability. Despite high revenue, we struggled with managing expenses. Faced with the "Loss" fear, my biggest problem "ish"—self-avoidance—showed up. It wasn't until I faced this directly that growth became possible. I practiced removing self-avoidance and replacing it with the ability to act, then affirmed: *I am taking action*, and I followed through. I sought support, joined a business group, and found a mentor. Accepting help was transformational.

But this wasn't just about business. It was a mirror for personal growth. Like business, personal development requires constant reassessment. I embraced daily practice and recognized and redirected other "ishes" beyond self-avoidance, self-importance, and self-righteousness. I'd identified that self-reliance limited me greatly. I thought I had to do it all, be everywhere, and carry it alone. That mindset not only affected my leadership but also strained relationships at home. I had to accept help, learn how to delegate, and practice trust.

Daily mindfulness helped me recognize the storm "flares" as they happened. And with each setback, I practiced redirecting my thinking, taking ownership of my actions, and learning from the impact my "ishes" had on others. Most importantly, I had to be patient with myself and my progress.

Leaning into leadership, I realized, is an inside job. And leadership isn't just a title. We all lead in our lives. I was the leader in my family, the chief provider, the caretaker, the business builder. But even with those roles, my "ishes" wreaked havoc until I learned to pause, reflect, and redirect.

Tools in Practice

Breathe, Then Think and Do the Opposite

Have you ever sat in a meeting and felt tension rise in your chest? Your tone shifts, and suddenly you're reacting, not responding. For me, this happened often when my belief, *"nobody cares,"* was triggered. That resentment, rooted in early emotional neglect, would spark self-importance and self-righteousness when I felt unheard or misunderstood. In those moments, the practice is simple but powerful: Breathe. Then think and do the opposite. I would take a few deep breaths and silently affirm: "I'm removing self-importance and replacing it with humility. I'm open and receptive." Then, I'd offer acknowledgment to reset the tone and the connection.

One-Minute Meditation

You know the feeling: back-to-back meetings, no break in sight, and just when you get a moment, someone needs you—a child, a coworker, a partner. Your mind screams, "I can't get a minute to myself!" You try to set a boundary, but it's not respected. Frustration builds. Anger flares. The next thing you know, you're reacting then you feel bad about yourself afterwards.

Here's what helps: A one-minute meditation. Start by mentally affirming: "I'm removing anger and replacing it with calm. I'm calm." Then during the one minute, take a deep breath in while saying, "I'm breathing in calm," hold for three seconds, and exhale with, "I'm breathing out anger." Repeat twice more, then affirm: "I'm centered. I'm calm. I'm handling demands."

These are simple practices, but with vigilance and consistency, they become your go-to tools. Over time, they help you stay grounded through daily turbulence. And the more you practice, the more progress you'll feel. Contentment isn't sudden. It builds with every redirected thought and every small act of self-awareness.

Owning Your Worth

I'd made tremendous progress, but it took one more moment to fully recognize my worth. Five years into the business, we pitched a privately owned UK-based start-up. After our presentation, the billionaire owner invited us for a follow-up meeting. As we sat across the boardroom table, he directed his questions to me. At first, I was stunned. Is he really asking for *my* opinion? Fear crept in, and I thought, *I'm not qualified to answer that!* But I caught it. I removed the fear and affirmed: I'm capable. I'd remembered what I learned from Jeffers and repeated it in my mind: *Act as if. You've got this, girl.*

We won the business. But more importantly, I finally owned my value. On the flight home, I reflected: If a billionaire sees my worth, why don't I? In that moment, I claimed it—I'm the CEO. And from then on, I used that title.

This is the lesson so many professional women need to hear. Your fear and your "ish" thinking are what holds you back. Not your title. Not your experience. Not what anyone else thinks. Declaring your worth is vital. No one can do it for you. Others may affirm your value, but until you believe it and live it, nothing changes.

Fulfillment isn't found in titles or achievements. It's built from the inside out. It starts with patience, recognizing when fear and self-centered thinking is holding us back, and learning to redirect. The more you redirect, the more esteem you build. The more esteem you build, the more at peace you feel. And that peace? That's what true contentment is all about.

Lesson 3: Practicing Vigilance with Support Fosters Accountability

Have you ever been in a meeting at work where your manager became frustrated, took a tone, and you felt berated and publicly humiliated? Then you silently seethed and spoke to everyone you knew who reports to the manager to commiserate how horrible they were?

I'm coaching someone who'd had the same experience and allowed me to share this with you. She'd completed The Turnaround and recognized how her unresolved resentment led to meltdowns when she didn't feel understood. And when she felt unheard, she became impatient and dismissive. She'd made great progress at home and at work and was feeling content until she encountered a storm: Her manager became frustrated and took a tone during a team meeting.

Her unresolved resentment triggered, "I'm not good enough" followed by her "Never" fear. She'd been reduced to a puddle, and rather than asserting herself with her manager following the meeting, she'd been consumed with self-pity and self-seeking. Crying, she'd sent a message to a colleague who'd been at the meeting to cancel the next one because she'd been too upset to talk. This action prompted her colleague to call her, at which point, she began seeking validation about her performance.

In the chapter "Eye of the Storm," you learned how we're often unaware of the impact that our actions have on others. This is a great example of how the manager's storm became the triggering event for the woman in this example.

Despite her progress, she was emotionally distraught and felt like a failure. She struggled to turn it around and went right back to "ish" thinking and behavior. As we talked it through, she identified the cause: Her esteem was threatened. She hadn't used "think and do the opposite" or the one-minute meditation when her storm started. Since she'd succumbed to the fear and included other colleagues and subordinates in her storm, we looked at the Connection Builder for direction on how she was going to address the situation and do an esteem-able act.

Example from her Connection Builder

Who	How am I hurtful or unkind?	What esteemable act can I do?	How will I do this?
Manager	Gossiped and said unkind things.	Acknowledge, seek to understand by asking what he thinks the disconnect is.	Schedule a meeting. Affirm I am good enough and capable.
Colleague	Gossiped and said unkind things.	Acknowledge.	Schedule a brief call.

We practiced the acknowledgement conversation she'd have with her manager. And when she followed through with it the next day, he immediately acknowledged her contributions and value. He told her about the challenges he'd been facing related to value creation with the client, which gave her understanding about the pressure he was under. Then they spent time discussing the problem and brainstorming potential solutions.

Following the meeting, she'd realized she'd reacted to his storm.

By practicing emotional accountability and vigilance with a Life Storm Buddy, we become more aware when we're stuck in self-centered thinking. In this example, taking action helped her realize that her manager's behavior wasn't a reflection of her performance. And through acknowledgment, she gained understanding of his challenges and opened the door to deeper connection. She also clarified the situation with her colleague and offered positive feedback about her manager.

Practicing vigilance with support helps lift us out of the self-centered fog, guiding us toward action, clarity, and meaningful connection.

Lesson 4: Personal Growth is a Daily Choice

Have you ever felt amazing on your personal growth journey, as if you were standing on entirely new ground, handling challenges differently, often better than ever before? That is, until another storm strikes?

I have.

In my journey, I'd felt good about my progress personally and professionally. So good, I started to back off from my practices—although I didn't realize I was doing that. I felt secure inside, and while I didn't always manage things as well as I wanted, I held on to the progress I'd made with my "ish" behavior. Things felt stable.

Then the storm clouds started rolling in, followed by a category 5 hurricane.

Our industry underwent a major transformation, threatening our company's existence if we didn't adapt and innovate quickly. Amid that pressure, we learned that our finance leader, who'd driven our growth and profitability, had a rare brain disease that took her life within a year.

Fear took me by storm all over again. I became a plow, running down anyone who got in the way. I found myself back to the place I was more than a decade prior when I'd been fired. My "ishes" were back in full force and volcanic eruptions were frequent. I was dismissive and upsetting people, and I was angry when people didn't do what I'd asked them to do. I was at a new crossroads for growth. I had the Aurora Method tools but resisted applying acknowledgement in the professional setting, fearing I would look weak as a leader.

I'd made strides at work because I'd been practicing and was patient with myself. I'd put the straw down and was grateful for all that I had. I'd been managing the leadership roles across my life, and I'd been content.

So, what happened? I'd stopped my daily practice, AGAIN! I'd stopped the pivotal practice for sustained change and growth: vigilance. My daily practice shifted from intention to checking the boxes. At night, I quickly reviewed my day, manifested and affirmed some, but I'd stopped my morning intention. And I was back to blaming everyone for our problems.

As we know, it had nothing to do with them. I was living in fear and lack and knew I had to get back to daily practice to get past it. Yet, I got angry at the thought of it. *Why? Why does this keep happening? Don't you ever get to a point where it just goes away?*

No. It doesn't.

Self-centred thinking and behavior are our default in the face of inner turbulence or a major life storm, and unless we remain vigilant, we'll find ourselves just like we were before, sometimes worse.

I'd stopped practicing, and without vigilance, I'd slipped back into self-centered thinking. I felt misunderstood, criticized, opposed, and rejected. In the face of professional relationship struggles, I defaulted to JADE: justifying my meticulousness, arguing for my way, defending my actions, and explaining my decisions. Instead of seeking to understand, I was focused on being understood—and that created distance.

I had a setback in my progress and had to face the truth of what I'd become in the presence of my "Loss" and "Never" fear. I became the storm again, rather than being the leader who needed to be the calm in it. I turned back to the Aurora Method.

When we find ourselves stuck or struggling again, we simply go back to the Self-Assessment and Turnaround and write down who or what we're angry with and follow the Self-Assessment process. Then we complete The Turnaround to see where fear has taken our thinking and what is really threatened, so we can look at our Life Storm Navigator to see if we've previously identified the "ish" or trait. And if so, we can ask, is it consistent with how we're acting now? If not, we can identify the new trait and trait behavior and determine how we're going to change it, then develop our personal affirmations so we can think and do the opposite. We can then turn to the Connection Builder for guidance on who to restore connection with and implement the acknowledgement conversations.

Personal growth isn't a one-time achievement. It's a daily choice.

Contentment can be deceptive, making vigilance essential in mindfulness practice. By staying aware of unresolved resentment triggers, fear, and self-centered thinking, we can redirect our thoughts and behaviors, responding with intention rather than reacting. With patience and consistent effort, these small daily practices shape who we become, fostering deeper connection and inner peace.

And yes, we are all busy! I understand how much you're managing and how it feels like there's no extra time for mindfulness. But here's the thing: Mindfulness isn't another task on your to-do list—it's self-care—a tool that helps you handle everything with more clarity and calm and builds esteem along the way. As we've reviewed, even just a few moments a day can shift how you experience stress, make decisions, and connect with those around you. You don't need more time. You just need small, intentional pauses that take you out of the fog. And over time, practice strengthens your ability to respond, allowing you to sustain growth and contentment amid life's daily storms.

"Resilience begins the moment you stop resisting your storms—and start listening to what they're trying to teach you."

—Tracy Doyle

Navigating the Turbulent Sky
Resilience in Practice

Resilience. The ability to adapt, recover, and grow stronger in the face of challenges, struggles, setbacks, or adversity. Resilience doesn't come from pushing through or pretending everything's fine. It begins when you stop fighting what's hard. Our struggles aren't obstacles, they're messengers.

Our storms continue. But whether it's unexpected turbulence in our daily lives or a category 3 hurricane caused by a life event, we've built a strong foundation from which we can continue to grow. The Aurora Method practices together with the tools empower us to navigate our way through with grace.

Practice 7 of the Aurora Method reminds us that we can adapt and face each setback on our journey with a powerful guiding principle: **When the struggles return, re-examine and enhance your daily mindfulness practices.** We learned about deceptive contentment in the previous chapter and how we may relax or stop our practices entirely. What we saw from the examples was how storm "flares"—our fear, seeking and "ish thinking"—return, reigniting old patterns of behavior.

Resilience isn't just about enduring hardship. It's about learning from it, shifting your mindset, and moving forward with greater wisdom and strength. True resilience is rooted in self-awareness, emotional flexibility, and the willingness to embrace change instead of resisting it. And one of the key lessons from deceptive contentment is that when we have a setback and old struggles resurface, it's a signal to return to our practices and to deepen them in order to keep growing.

Resilience is built through consistent practice, even when we falter. Setbacks aren't failures; they're invitations to deepen our awareness and refine our approach. And accepting the struggle is part of the journey. With daily mindfulness and vigilance as your compass, you can navigate life's turbulent skies by returning to your practices to stay grounded and continue your mindfulness journey.

Now, let's take a moment to reflect on how we can refine and strengthen our daily practices when the struggles return.

Start by assessing where in the Aurora Method you may have disengaged.

Ask yourself these four questions:

1. Have I been practicing the end-of-day reflection?
2. Have I been manifesting and affirming?
3. Have I been starting my day with the morning intention?
4. Have I been actively thinking and doing the opposite and doing one-minute meditations?

When we're in the struggle and answer no to all the questions, the guidance is to go back to the fundamentals of the Aurora Method:

- ☼ Begin with the Self-Assessment worksheet and examine the struggle. Write down who you're angry with or who hurt you. Complete the row as you've done previously.
- ☼ Then complete The Turnaround and Turnaround statement(s) to identify the cause and your unresolved resentment, and fear and self-centered thinking that's triggered.
- ☼ Pull up your Life Storm Navigator. Are the traits (seeking, "ishes," and acts) on your list? If so, heed the guidance you've set for yourself before. If not, add it, then complete the opposites exercise.
- ☼ Reflect, then create your personal affirmation for this situation.
- ☼ Go to your Connection Builder for guidance on how to improve the relationship.
- ☼ Prepare, then implement your approach to acknowledgement.

Now let's explore what to do when you've disengaged from certain Aurora Method practices.

Stopped the End-of-day Reflection

When we stop or quickly check the box with the end-of-day reflection, we often miss the opportunities to practice manifesting and affirming. You may likely have answered no to the second question as well. The simplicity of the end of day reflection, "how did I do?" coupled with being busy may lead to what I call Teflon answers, or evading taking the time to go deep with the question. When in Teflon answer mode, you may quickly answer, "I did well. Nothing major is going on. I'm good." But from experience, the farther we move away from taking time during the end-of-day reflection, the closer we get to unexpected turbulence and struggles.

We can enhance this exercise by having a quiet conversation with ourselves that builds on the original question: "How did I do today?" Add: "Do I owe anyone an apology?" This question quickly leads us to pause and do an honest assessment. "I did well—oh wait, I was short with my husband this morning, and he was distant during dinner." As you can see, the additional question takes you back to the Aurora Method, because once you see the struggle, you naturally want to identify the opportunities to acknowledge, mend, build esteem, and nourish.

If needed, refer to the fundamentals of the Aurora Method outlined above, as it will quickly provide the path forward to implementing change.

Follow the daily review as outlined to get you quickly back on track.

The Daily Review: A Practice for Growth and Accountability

\	The Daily Review Reflection
How did I do?	Do I owe anyone an apology? If yes, what did I do?
Identify Traits	What traits were triggered (fear, seeking, "ishes," acts)?
Manifest	Replace trait with the opposite.
Affirm	Affirm the opposite.

What esteemable act can I do? How will I do it?	How could I have handled it? What needs to be acknowledged?
Acknowledge	Practice the conversation.
Implement	Follow through with the acknowledgement conversation.

Adding this daily practice enhances your growth and, over time, fosters accountability by encouraging honesty with yourself and allowing you to address challenges as they arise or soon after. The questions become second nature, thinking and doing the opposite feels intuitive, and acknowledgement conversations feel natural.

Stopped the Morning Intention

Many women I coach stay consistent with their evening practices—reviewing the day, manifesting, and affirming before bed—but often skip the morning intention. The most common reasons? Too many demands or simply feeling too tired. For many, the morning feels like a race because of juggling the kids' needs, getting everyone out the door, and mentally preparing for work, leaving no space for even a minute of stillness.

But just five minutes of quiet in the morning is not a luxury. It's a necessity. It serves two key purposes: connecting with yourself to set a positive tone for the day and practicing meaningful self-care. Those few minutes offer space to breathe, reflect, and realign your mindset before the noise of the day takes over.

When we skip this moment of mindfulness, we risk starting the day off reactive and ungrounded. Chaos creeps in more easily, clouding judgment and increasing stress. But when we begin the day centered and calm, we restore mental clarity and build the resilience needed to meet daily pressures with intention.

"But how do I find the time?" many ask.

Believe it or not, you can find the time when you examine your routine. In my personal journey, I woke up 15 minutes early to hit the snooze for 10 minutes, then found the 5 minutes. For a woman I'm coaching, she found the time while breastfeeding her baby. Another woman I coach is often met with her toddler waking her. Since getting up earlier would not be a guarantee, she found the time after the kids are dropped off, just before she starts work.

Embrace the idea of gifting yourself five minutes of quiet intention each morning.

The morning intention is about presence of mind. You were initially guided to breathe, express gratitude, manifest, affirm, and reflect. Shifting your mindset around time constraints and enhancing this practice is the first step toward reclaiming your well-being and inner peace.

Let's review how you can simplify this exercise.

After you've found five minutes, take one to two deep breaths. Then, thinking about your reflection from the night before, declare your affirmations for the day ahead. For example, "I'm centered, I'm calm. My day is free from fear. I'm enough. I'm embracing challenges as opportunities. I'm handling the demands with grace and kindness. I'm acknowledging (insert name), and I'm going to…(esteemable act). I'm embracing this day with joy."

Stay Accountable: Find Your Life Storm Buddy

As we've learned, self-centered thinking can cloud our perceptions. When fear takes the reins, it drives us through a city of limitations, leaving us feeling stuck and unable to break free. We've seen the consequences of complacency, making it even more essential to stay accountable to our daily practice—our key to growth, transformation, and connection. And we've learned that practicing alone may lead to deceptive contentment, the illusion that mindfulness was no longer needed. Yet, as the examples showed, inner disturbances return.

Vigilance, supported by an accountability partner, can be the key to staying the course. I encourage you to find a Life Storm Buddy, such as a trusted friend who practices personal growth. A Life Storm Buddy is someone who can help you navigate the journey with accountability and support. If you don't have anyone, consider joining our Aurora community.

The purpose of working with a Life Storm Buddy is to stay accountable to your daily practices, be honest about your storm "flares" and traits (seeking, "ishes," and acts), discuss your approach to acknowledgment, and confirm that you've followed through—practices that sustain and continue your growth and strengthen your relationships.

The question I'm often asked is, "How do you work with a Life Storm Buddy and how often?"

In my experience, a daily check-in is the most optimal but not necessary. Again, how do you find time?! This ten-minute commitment helps you practice vigilance daily. This heightened awareness helps you take responsibility for your actions rather

---

You don't have to do this alone. Visit www.tracydoyle.life if you need help.

than falling into autopilot or old JADE habits. Similar to how you examined your routine for the five minutes, I encourage you to do the same here.

Where can you find ten minutes in your day to gift yourself support and connection?

Once you've identified your buddy and gifted yourself the time, I suggest the check-in follow the "three G" format.

The Three G's: Glitches, Gifts, and Gratitude

The "three G" format helps you maximize time and get right to work. After your typical pleasantries, start your check-in call by addressing these questions:

1. What were my **glitches** (storm "flares") today?
   - ☼ Review what is occupying your mind—the event or events that led to your flare—and share what happened.
   - ☼ What traits did you identify (seeking, "ishes" or acts)? Share them.

If you didn't have any storm flares, share that too and proceed to the next question.

2. What were my **gifts** today (my ability to see what needs to change or how I successfully redirected negative thinking)? If you had a flare, do the following:
   - ☼ Knowing your traits, review your opposites and what needs to be acknowledged.
   - ☼ Discuss your approach to acknowledgement and practice.
   - ☼ Commit to when you plan to implement.

3. What am I **grateful** for?

   ☼ Now, find three things from the day you're grateful for.

By staying vigilant with your Life Storm Buddy, you can recognize when you're avoiding difficult truths, making excuses, or slipping back into self-centered thinking. It allows you to course-correct and make intentional choices that support your personal growth and relationships. Ultimately, vigilance with accountability ensures your daily mindfulness practice translates into meaningful change rather than remaining just an intention.

Life storms persist, but with steady practice and a Life Storm Buddy, you can navigate the turbulence with grace and find yourself living in the clear sky.

"We are not human
beings having a
spiritual experience;
we are spiritual
beings having
a human experience."

— Pierre Teilhard de Chardin

Living in Your Clear Sky

Freedom. The state of being unrestricted or, as we've learned, the ability to navigate life without being controlled by our past wounds, limiting beliefs, or unprocessed emotions. It's not about erasing pain but about releasing its hold on your present and future.

The Aurora Method has shown you how to identify the triggering event—your unresolved resentments—created by how you internalized your life experiences, freeing you to build or restore connection with those who matter to you. You've learned how to engage challenges rather than being ruled by your triggers. You know how to respond, not react. You've embraced mindfulness, and practicing vigilance has enabled you to understand the impact of your actions on others, empowering you to seek to understand first, fostering harmony and connection in your daily life. You've found peace in imperfection, accepting that change is an ongoing process, not a destination. You're becoming the change that you want to be and living authentically, free from fear, free from lack, and free from discontentment.

You're reclaiming your power, letting go of old beliefs, and stepping into life with openness, resilience, and a sense of inner peace. You feel connected and believe emotional fulfillment is attainable and real.

Life storms continue though. Having stripped away the power of our unresolved resentment and softening their impact on our thinking and behavior, we're free to go deeper. Free to receive the abundance we're manifesting in our lives. Free to be content.

Freedom takes courage. As Frederick Douglass, the famous abolitionist, said, "If there is no struggle, there is no progress." Although he was fighting to overcome the bondage of slavery, we must continue to overcome the bondage of our self-centered thinking. And when we have the willingness to break through self-centeredness, we *can* be free. Free to make choices and take actions that boost our esteem and self-worth. Free to change the trajectory of our lives with the people we love in it.

We're no longer humans doing, we're humans *being*. Free to be courageous. To speak our truth, express our needs, disengage from the who's right fight and commit to what's right. We're free to be.

While embracing freedom, I kept returning to the same inner turmoil, trapped in old beliefs that kept me stuck in victim thinking: *I can't say no to my mother. She needs me because she can't manage on her own. No one else can help, only I can. I have to do it all; it's my responsibility.*

Despite all the growth and years of practice, I continued to be a human doing and remained stuck in the struggle with my family. It felt like constant static in the background, triggering me when I was searching for peace. I'd realized I had to keep examining and refining my daily practices, because my "Never" fear continued to ignite "ishes" that affected my relationship with my partner and within my professional life. My thinking remained limited, and as a result, I felt stuck, frustrated, and disappointed in myself.

Through deeper reflection, the message became clear. I had to stay committed to my practices if I truly wanted freedom. I'd cleared enough of the noise to begin embracing that I was enough. I had the strength to kindly express and uphold boundaries. Yet still, I was afraid—afraid to let go of the responsibility I'd carried for my mother for so long.

Practice 7 encourages us to reexamine our daily practices, while Practice 8 declares that **daily mindfulness releases us from fear and the limitations of our thinking**. I returned to my routine with greater intention, gifting myself fifteen minutes of quiet each morning and expanding my morning intention. I incorporated walking meditation and deeper reflection, which became cornerstones in my continued growth and helped quiet the fear and limited thinking that once held me back.

In my quest for freedom, I affirmed: *I'm enough. I have done enough. I'm calm and strong enough to let go.* With this mindset, I found the courage to tell my mother, without anger, that it was time for her and my sister to take responsibility for themselves. It was emotionally difficult but deeply necessary.

When the day came, my mother tried to press every button she'd ever installed in me. The names, the expletives—too harsh to repeat—came pouring out. But I stayed quiet, grounded in my affirmations. My mind was clear, and I remained calm. At one point, she said, "You've had a bug up your ass about me for years. Why don't you just tell me what your problem is?"

That was the moment, and I seized it. I affirmed, *I'm centered, I'm calm*, and spoke my truth. I told my mother what professionals had said for years: She was mentally ill and had refused help. I made it clear that her children and grandchildren were her responsibility, not mine. Supporting everyone emotionally, physically, and financially was draining me and straining my relationship. I calmly explained the steps I was taking. She told me to go fuck myself and hung up.

I wasn't sure if that was progress or a setback, but my network said, "Great progress!" and my partner said, "Good job. You finally said it." I cried after I hung up, then left for work.

We didn't speak for two years.

The next day, I continued my morning routine and affirmed abundance. *I'm open and receptive to my family. My family is in my life. All is well.* This practice helped me to move away from lack and refrain from self-centered thinking and behavior.

Although letting go was painful, change happened. My mom was resourceful. She moved in with her companion, Barry. They moved to North Carolina. My sister, her husband, and her youngest daughter soon followed and moved in with them. The abundance I affirmed relieved me from the burden of family responsibility and gave me the freedom to focus on my relationship and career.

Without any effort on my part, my mom took steps to repair our relationship. My youngest niece was in a positive and somewhat stable environment Barry had created for her. I wasn't involved. Daily practice had, indeed, released me from the limitations of my thinking and enabled me to have a fulfilling relationship with my mom and my niece.

My mom and I returned to our weekly calls. I listened and was present, and I visited when I could. We enjoyed Sunday brunches or dinners, celebrated birthdays together, and created fun and positive memories. My heart was full. Although I continued to walk through life and its storms, I maintained an abundance mindset related to my family and the emotional fulfillment I gained was completely unexpected.

In 2017, I learned my mom had given up a baby girl for adoption when I was three years old. And my sister Lisa (same name as my other sister) found me! Then, in 2020, I found my father's children. My brother Bob, my sister Diane, and my sister Sue welcomed me to the family. I went from lack to overwhelming abundance.

Daily mindfulness helped me regain my footing during difficult challenges at work. It gave me the clarity to respond more thoughtfully and reduced how often I reacted to fear. Over time, it also helped me lead with greater presence and steadiness. I began to see how these practices don't just change how we feel but transform how we show up in every part of our lives.

Committing to mindfulness is a commitment to ourselves. Over time, it frees us from the grip of fear and limited thinking, allowing contentment to take root. That calm, centered presence—the one we thought we had to earn or chase—is already within us, and daily practice is how we return to it.

Early in my journey, I embraced Susan Jeffers' idea that to overcome fear, we must seek our Higher Self. Through the Aurora Method, I began to understand that it's fear rooted in self-centered thinking that clouds our clarity and blocks us from accessing our inner power. Daily mindfulness clears that fog. It sustains our well-being and reconnects us to the strength within.

From experience, I've learned that action is the foundational key to all success. We must clear the blocks, commit to practice, and with time, we can realize change isn't just possible—it's happening. As Glennon Doyle reminds us, *we can do hard things*.

And as my Pop once said, true growth—no matter the philosophy or faith—always leads us back to the soul. Every great teacher points us inward.

Acceptance and willingness are the keys to finding our clear sky.

It begins with accepting how our life experiences have shaped our thinking and being willing to examine them. Accepting that it's not them causing our angst but the inner disturbance creating the storm. Being willing to recognize, redirect, and acknowledge so we can mend and rebuild the bridges that connect us to the people in our lives.

It's accepting our humanness—our self-centered traits—and staying willing to watch for them, listen for them, and take responsibility. And when we recognize that we've been hurtful or unkind, we choose to make it right.

Mindfulness, then, becomes more than a tool. It becomes a spiritual practice that connects us deeply to ourselves and others.

With daily practice and the Aurora Method, we now hold the tools to navigate our storms and return to peace, no matter what arises.

Does this mean we become perfect beings? Absolutely not! Far from it.

Some of my greatest lessons have come from the everyday people in my life—friends and family—who, like all of us, are navigating their own struggles. But when we stay open and curious, we can learn so much from the mindfulness practices others have embraced to free themselves from fear and limited thinking on their journeys.

From my Aunt Ann, I learned the value of prayer and reflection. My friend Candace taught me affirmative prayer. My friend Missy reminded me that daily walks can quiet the mind and connect us to the power within. My friend Brenda taught me that acceptance truly is the answer to most struggles, and when I'm disturbed, I now pause and ask, *what am I not accepting?* Her wisdom helps me return to my practice and reset.

As you build your support network, engage with those who are also seeking growth. We're all learning how to break through fear and self-centered thinking. Our paths may differ, but our desire to grow is the same.

Living in your clear sky doesn't mean the storms stop. It means you now have the tools to fly through them. Like a pilot adjusting to unexpected turbulence, you can pause, reflect, redirect, and chart your way back to the clear sky.

Commit. Become a resilience champion.

As navigators through life's storms, we must strive to be resilience champions—people who embody strength, adaptability, and perseverance in the face of adversity. We don't just endure challenges. We transform them into opportunities for growth, inspiring others along the way. We navigate setbacks without being defined by them. We acknowledge our struggles without becoming them. We choose to learn, adapt, and rise.

As resilience champions, we live in our clear sky. We stay rooted in the Aurora Method, seeking constructive ways to move forward. We are solution-oriented, growth-minded, and grounded in compassion. We support and uplift others, sharing our wisdom and tools so they, too, can build resilience.

We're courageous. We're authentic. We show up, even when it's hard. We face life's storms with grace, grit, and purpose.

A Resilience Champion doesn't avoid hardship, we rise through it. We turn struggle into strength and help others do the same.

Let's keep rising—together.

Our journey doesn't end here. As we grow, we inevitably face hardships. But we now know that struggle isn't something to fear. It's a signal for progress. The more we practice, the more we release fear and the limiting beliefs that hold us back.

I want to leave you with two final stories that reflect this truth.

Accepting Limitations to Find Freedom

In 2018, our company faced a significant financial crisis. We'd struggled to replace the talent of our financial leader we'd lost years earlier, and we were confronted by it. I was gripped by "Loss," "Less," and "Never" fear, anger, self-deprecation, and self-pity.

I stood at a crossroads: shut down the business or do what it takes. Rising meant hard decisions. It meant laying off half the company. It meant admitting my limitations and accepting that the business outgrew my skills. It meant stepping aside as a leader.

My default was to collapse emotionally, but I turned to the Aurora Method, my mindfulness practice, and a quote from Braque Talley, PhD that I read on social media: "If you accept the call to leadership, you must be willing to be misunderstood, criticized, opposed, accused, and even rejected." Rising meant facing every fear and limiting belief I had and embracing the idea that successful entrepreneurs build on failure and use it to succeed.

Daily practice helped me redirect the ongoing storm flares and setbacks. I stayed present, practiced one-minute meditation, think and do the opposite, and identified and applied new affirmations to manage through self-centered thinking. Eventually, a former employee called with an opportunity that brought us a new leader, someone who led us to a successful exit.

Accepting my limitations truly gave me freedom—both financially and emotionally.

Freedom to Change and Serve

Just a week before launching the new leadership team, my mom passed away. I was in the middle of two major life storms: letting go of my company and grieving my mother. But what followed was unexpected. I came to understand that my sister was not just struggling—she was disabled, and her needs far exceeded anything I'd imagined.

Grief gave way to anger, then to the belief, "I'm not worthy of freedom," a new resentment I uncovered. This belief ignited my "Never" fear again: *I'll never be free from caretaking the mentally ill in my family.* I realized I'd deceived myself into thinking I could manage her care from afar. I returned to work, but emotionally, I was adrift and back in the tumultuous sea. As a passenger on the ship, I struggled to find my place. The process of letting go was harder than I thought as I steered through each negative thought, each fear, and each "act." I leaned on Practice 7, enhancing my routine with walking meditations, deeper affirmations focused on acceptance and understanding, and daily reflection.

Then we were all in a global tsunami—COVID-19—and gripped by the "Loss" fear. Peoples "ishes" and acts were flaring like fireworks, and mental health crises were abounded, my sister's included. Her neighbor and our family friend had expressed concerns. As the pandemic persisted, my niece had the courage to tell me she needed help with her mom. That reality hit hard, as my youngest niece had assumed the same caretaker role as I had, and at the same age.

I could Forget Everything and Run and avoid dealing with it or Face Everything and Rise. I had to squarely face two persistent "ishes:" self-deception and self-avoidance.

Isn't it funny how "ishes" keep turning up? This is why daily practice is so important!

To rise meant to uproot my life and move to South Carolina where my sister and niece lived while my partner remained in New Jersey. To rise meant to accept this hardship on our relationship and provide my niece with the opportunity to thrive. But my partner, the gentlest of souls said, "It's okay. I'm not going anywhere." And her love and understanding gave me the courage and strength to serve my family.

Uprooting my life to caretake was overwhelming. I was reactive. But I wasn't alone.

A support network is the greatest gift you can give yourself. And with the support of my network and daily practices, we built structure and stability and addressed years of neglected health. And my niece began to thrive.

Still, the storms continued. Old triggers flared. I caught myself "JADEing," falling into old patterns and struggling with relationships. I'd been practicing acceptance and found the Serenity Prayer, a useful tool throughout my day. I used it in meetings often when I didn't feel heard. I would quietly say it and use it to redirect my thinking and stay grounded: *God, grant me the serenity to accept the things I cannot change*—I can't change this person's opinion—*the courage to change the things I can*—I can listen. I am centered, I am calmly acknowledging—*and the wisdom to know the difference*. A very effective and intentional minute.

When the big day finally came, and the business sold, I felt both elated and afraid. No income was daunting, and new challenges at home surfaced. My sister started having difficulty swallowing from the bipolar disorder medication. After multiple changes, she'd been given older, less effective medications which didn't address her frequent manic and depressive cycles.

I felt emotionally drained and at my wit's end. The loud, nonstop talking, the days in bed, the combativeness, and the hurt and betrayal she caused while struggling with poorly managed bipolar disorder reopened old wounds. Like my mother, she weaponized the things we'd talk about—or what she overheard in conversations—to hurt me over a perceived injustice. And my reactions were intense. Run or rise?

I had to rise again. And this time, the key was forgiveness.

I'd accepted that it was her mental illness, not her, that causes the hurt and pain. I found a simple letting-go prayer from *A Course in Miracles*: "I forgive you. I release you to the Universe." Repeating it gave me strength to transition her to assisted living and find peace.

Forgiveness gave me the ability to stay the course. As of this writing, one of the most rewarding experiences has been supporting my niece as she navigates her senior year of high school and transition to college. We talk openly, and I share what I've learned so she can grow with confidence and claim her own freedom sooner. Watching this once-struggling child as she uncovers her strengths, realizes her potential, and thrives has been a profound gift.

Through this experience, I transitioned from CEO to resilience champion. I found inner peace and purpose.

And now, I'm here to share the wisdom that helped me with other overwhelmed professionals who feel burned out and disconnected. We all have our stories. We've all been wounded. And we all struggle. My mission is to help you recognize and redirect the self-centered thinking created by your life experiences so that you can restore connection to yourself and find fulfillment in your relationships.

This is the promise of the Aurora Method and daily practice—true freedom to grow, to embrace change, and to serve the people in our lives with love, acceptance, understanding, kindness, and joy.

"Never underestimate the
power you have to
take your life in
a new direction."

— Germany Kent

Views for Your Life's Horizon

Now, let's turn toward your life's horizon—the beginning of a new frontier, filled with possibility. With an open mind and a fresh perspective, where does your path lead from here?

Transformation is always possible. And with daily mindfulness and the practices from the Aurora Method, here are the promises you've begun to realize:

- ☼ You've come to understand that we're all wounded by the life experiences we've internalized. Fear and self-centered thinking fuel our struggles, creating barriers to meaningful connection.
- ☼ You've opened your mind and accepted that when you recognize and redirect your thoughts, you change your life.
- ☼ You've faced hard truths and accepted your role in the struggle. You're choosing to break free from fear and self-centered thinking so you can experience deeper connection and fulfillment—at home, at work, and within yourself.

- ☼ You've let go of resentment. You've embraced new ways of thinking that build self-esteem and emotional security from the inside out.

- ☼ You understand that successful relationships are a shared responsibility. By practicing acknowledgment and building bridges, you've restored meaningful connections.

- ☼ You're committed to daily mindfulness and vigilance. You trust the process, and you're patient with your progress.

- ☼ You've learned to celebrate your growth, knowing setbacks are part of being human. And you choose to rise every time.

- ☼ You've discovered that true peace and contentment come from within through consistent practice, and you've committed to living that truth daily.

You've found freedom and happiness. You're becoming the person you want to be.

My Aspirational Vision for You

Through your journey with the Aurora Method, you've gained a deep, intuitive understanding of life and its storms, that we've all been wounded, and we all struggle to break through the fog. But we don't have to do it alone. With your Life Storm Buddy and support network, you've experienced firsthand that everyday people can uplift and guide one another. We grow stronger together.

So here's my vision for your Life's Horizon:

You are now a Resilience Champion. A Life Storm Navigator. You carry the wisdom to guide others toward their clear sky. The journey doesn't end here—it grows. Because together, we can create a ripple of hope and change.

Let's lift one another, support those still in the storm, and remind every woman who feels empty or unseen that connection, purpose, and fulfillment are possible.

Join me. And let's rise *together*.

Let's Stay Connected

Embracing change and committing to The Aurora Method and its mindfulness practices may feel daunting at first, but remember: *Every transformation begins with a single step*. If you're ready and want to create real, lasting change in your life it's time. Time to give yourself permission for it, time to ask for help with it, and time to receive support so that you can go for it!

Go to www.tracydoyle.life to explore how we can guide you through every step of the Aurora Method. Accountability to your thinking is critical for sustained growth. Join us on this journey and let's grow together!

Follow us on social media

- www.linkedin.com/in/tracy-doyle-aurora-co/
- www.facebook.com/profile.php?id=61574790167885
- @tracydoyle.life

Resources

This section provides comprehensive support materials and blank copies of each of the Aurora Method Tools:

The Self-Assessment

The Turnaround

The Life Storm Navigator

The Connection Builder

You can recreate them in your journal, or you can go to www.tracydoyle.life/Resources and download them.

And remember, if you need support or help along the way, visit www.tracydoyle.life to learn more how we can support you on your journey.

The Self-Assessment

Column 1	Column 2	Column 3					
Who?	**What did they do?**	**How did this affect me?**					
		Safety & Financial Security	Emotional Security	Personal Relations	Intimate Relations	Esteem	Ambitions

The Self-Assessment

Column 4	Column 5				
What did I do?	**My actions were...**				
	Self-Seeking	Self-"ish"	Dishonest	Thoughtless	Afraid

Self-Assessment Support Material

Column 3: Definitions

Safety and Financial Security

Sense of safety in your surroundings and security related to material well-being, (ie., having a roof over your head, heated home, having running water to bathe, food to eat, clothes to wear, etc).

Emotional Security

Sense of security related to emotional well-being, (ie., feeling loved, feeling accepted, or feeling confident rather than needing constant reassurance, etc).

Personal Relations

Sense of well-being, belonging, and acceptance by others (ie., friends, relatives, work colleagues).

Intimate Relations

Sense of well-being, belonging, and acceptance by intimate partner.

Esteem

Feeling confident in your own worth or abilities, self-respect, and feeling liked by others.

Ambitions

A desire to do or to achieve something, for example what I want for myself or others.

Resources   255

Self-Assessment Support Material

"Examine your actions" (Column 5) Definitions

Self-seeking

The act of prioritizing one's own desires, needs, or interests—often at the expense of others. It involves seeking validation, recognition, or personal gain without considering the impact on relationships or the well-being of others. While not always intentional, self-seeking behavior can manifest as manipulation, attention-seeking, or an excessive focus on personal outcomes rather than mutual connection and understanding.

Self-"ish"

Throughout the book, we refer to self-centered thinking as our core problem and have refined the term selfish to focus on the "ish" or variety of feelings, behaviors, and thoughts, that follow the word self. The list below is by no means exhaustive and is provided as a guide to help you complete column 5. In the event you do not identify with any of the definitions, google your behaviors and ask "what would you call this behavior_____ (describe it)?"

Once you have landed on your "ish" be sure to assign a code to it for use in *The Turnaround*.

© 2025 Tracy Doyle

The "Ishes"

Self-Avoidance	Distracting oneself or resisting self-examination to avoid facing uncomfortable emotions, thoughts, or responsibilities. It often manifests as procrastination, denial, numbing behaviors, or staying excessively busy to escape deeper personal truths.
Self-Condemnation	Harsh and relentless judgment of oneself; self-criticism or blaming oneself; where mistakes or shortcomings are viewed as personal failures rather than learning opportunities.
Self-Deception	The act of misleading oneself to avoid uncomfortable truths, painful emotions, or personal responsibility. This often involves downplaying problems, shifting blame to external factors, or ignoring the consequences of one's actions
Self-Deprecation	The act of undervaluing or belittling oneself, often through negative self-talk, humor, or dismissing one's abilities and achievements; constantly putting oneself down.
Self-Doubt	Uncertainty or lack of confidence in one's abilities, decisions, or worth. Questioning one's capabilities or value.
Self-Effacing	The tendency to downplay one's abilities, achievements, or importance to avoid attention or appearing boastful. This often involves deliberately minimizing personal contributions and prioritizing others' needs over one's own.
Self-Importance	An inflated sense of one's own importance, often expressed through arrogance, entitlement, condescension, dismissiveness, dominance, or lack of empathy. It manifests as a tendency to prioritize personal needs and opinions over those of others, often at the expense of meaningful connection and mutual respect.
Self-Justification	The act of defending one's actions, decisions, or beliefs by making excuses or shifting blame to avoid guilt and accountability.
Self-Loathing	Self-hatred, guilt, or worthlessness, manifesting as harsh self-judgment, feelings of unworthiness, and difficulty accepting love, success, or kindness from others.

Self-Pity	Excessive focus on one's own hardships, struggles, or perceived misfortunes, often accompanied by feelings of helplessness and victimhood.
Self-Reliance	Reliance on one's own efforts and abilities often manifesting as a reluctance to seek or accept help; a strong need to handle everything independently, not trusting others, and difficulty opening up or expressing vulnerability.
Self-Righteousness	A sense of moral or intellectual superiority, often accompanied by judgment, rigidity, and an unwillingness to consider other perspectives. Believe one's views, values, or actions are inherently right, while dismissing or looking down on those who disagree.

Dishonesty. Comes in two forms: knowingly making a false statement or lying by omission, which means withholding the truth when it should be shared, even if not directly ask. In this exercise, we are examining dishonesty in relation to fear's fight or flight response. When in "flight" we may lie to avoid confrontation.

Thoughtlessness. Acting without consideration, awareness, or regard for how one's words or actions affect others. It manifests as carelessness or failing to acknowledge or dismiss another's feelings, efforts, or boundaries, impulsiveness by interrupting or saying something without thought of the consequences, and lack of empathy or making insensitive comments. We examine thoughtlessness in relation to fear's fight or flight response. When in "fight" we may exhibit one or more of the traits associated with thoughtlessness.

Fear. An unpleasant feeling triggered by the perception of danger, real or imagined. There are many fears and for our purposes we are focused on three primary fears: **LOSS**: Fear of losing what we have, **LESS**: Fear of being or getting less than we desire, and **NEVER**: Fear of never getting what we want.

The Turnaround
My Needs

How did my life experiences affect me? (Check all that apply)

- ☐ Safety and financial security were threatened.
- ☐ Emotional security was threatened.
- ☐ Social belonging related to relationships with others was threatened.
- ☐ Social belonging related to relationships with love interests was threatened.
- ☐ Social belonging related to my being liked by others and myself was threatened.
- ☐ Ambitions were threatened.

Looking at your need patterns, describe what you see about yourself?

The Turnaround
My Fears

How have my life experiences affected fear? Looking at your fear patterns, what are your primary fears? (Select the fears that were most consistently noted on your *Self-Assessment*. It's okay if all three were selected equally.)

☐ **LOSS:** Fear of losing what we have

What do you do most in the presence of this fear? (check one)

☐ I'm thoughtless. I don't think about how my actions affect others.

☐ I'm dishonest. I outright tell a lie or I lie by omission (not saying anything at all).

☐ **LESS**: Fear of being or getting less than we desire

What do you do most in the presence of this fear? (check one)

☐ I'm thoughtless. I don't think about how my actions affect others.

☐ I'm dishonest. I outright tell a lie or I lie by omission (not saying anything at all).

☐ **NEVER:** Fear of never getting what we want

What do you do most in the presence of this fear? (check one)

☐ I'm thoughtless. I don't think about how my actions affect others.

☐ I'm dishonest. I outright tell a lie or I lie by omission (not saying anything at all).

The Turnaround
My Thinking

How does my fear fuel my thinking? Looking at your patterns, what are your primary self-centered thinking patterns? (Select seeking and the "ishes" that were noted as the most consistent on your *Self-Assessment*.)

Note: This exercise is personal to you. Should the "ishes" listed not include an "ish" you've identified, please note it or any others in the 'Other' section.

- ☐ Self-avoidance
- ☐ Self-condemnation
- ☐ Self-deception
- ☐ Self-deprecation
- ☐ Self-doubt
- ☐ Self-effacing
- ☐ Self-importance

- ☐ Self-justification
- ☐ Self-loathing
- ☐ Self-pity
- ☐ Self-reliance
- ☐ Self-righteousness
- ☐ Self-seeking

Other:

The Turnaround
My Behavior

How does my thinking affect how I act? Looking at your behavior, what are your common behavior patterns? (Select the behavior patterns most consistent as noted on your *Self-Assessment*.)

Note: This exercise is personal to you. Should the "behavior" listed not include something you've identified, please note it or any others in the 'Other' section.

- ☐ Angry
- ☐ Argumentative
- ☐ Arrogant
- ☐ Blame
- ☐ Complain
- ☐ Condescending
- ☐ Demanding
- ☐ Defensive
- ☐ Dishonest
- ☐ Dismissive
- ☐ Envious
- ☐ Gossip

- ☐ Impatient
- ☐ Indecisive
- ☐ Isolated
- ☐ Jealous
- ☐ Judgmental
- ☐ Negative
- ☐ Noncommitted
- ☐ Opinionated
- ☐ Overcommitted
- ☐ Prideful
- ☐ Procrastinate
- ☐ Voiceless (don't speak up)

Other:

© 2025 Tracy Doyle

Make The Turnaround

Complete The Turnaround Statement

When I am gripped by _____ fear, I'm _____ and my
(loss, less, or never)   (thoughtless or dishonest)

thinking is absorbed with _____.
                          ("ish and/or seeking")

When I'm _____ I _____.
         ("ish and/or seeking")   (insert the behavior from "What Did I Do?" (column 4))

Then I _____ and _____.
       (Insert the behavior from column 4 and corresponding "ish")   (Insert the behavior from column 4 and corresponding "ish")

I do this because my _____ were threatened.
                     (needs)

© 2025 Tracy Doyle

The Turnaround
Recognize Resentment

Repetitive behavior	Fear	Seeking or "Ishes"	What needs were threatened?	When did it start?	What belief did you internalize?

© 2025 Tracy Doyle

The Life Storm Navigator

LIFE STORM NAVIGATOR				
What Needs to Change?	How Do I Change?	What Needs to Change?	How Do I Change?	Manifest Change New Thought
Trait	Opposite	Trait Behavior	Opposite	Affirm

© 2025 Tracy Doyle

Life Storm Navigator Guide

The guide below lists potential character traits that you may have identified. Examples of opposites and affirmations are provided as a thought starter. Google and read about the "ishes" and the behavior you identified to guide you on developing your affirmations.

Remember, the *Life Storm Navigator* is your tool and needs to reflect only the traits and behaviors that you've identified and what opposites you want to manifest. Making your affirmation as personal to you as possible is the most effective way to manifest change.

Trait	Opposite	Trait Behavior	Opposite	Affirm
Self-avoidance	Take action	Avoid, distract myself complain, eat.	Take action, be honest, focus.	I am taking action.
Self-condemnation	Praise and nourish	Blame myself for everything that goes wrong. "It's all my fault, I'm a failure."	Pause when I am blaming or berating myself and redirect with affirmation.	I am good enough. I am safe, I am kind, I am able to work this through.
Self-deception	Get honest with myself	I believe that I can do it all.	Be honest when I'm overwhelmed. Accept my limitations.	I am truthful. I am accepting my limitations.
Self-deprecation	Nourish	Negative self-talk. "I don't know what I'm doing, I suck."	Listen for critical thoughts and say No, then affirm.	I am good enough; I am smart, I am capable and I am worthy of this...
Self-doubt	Confidence	Paralysis. Inability to focus. "I can't do this."	Identify 2 things that I can do. Affirm I can.	I am calm, I am confident, I am capable, I can do...
Self-effacing	Accept praise	Dismiss and give others credit.	Smile and say thank you.	I am safe, I am comfortable, I am accepting praise.

© 2025 Tracy Doyle

Trait	Opposite	Trait Behavior	Opposite	Affirm
Self-importance	Interest in others	Dismissive, arrogant, condescending. "I'll show you what I know!"	Remain quiet, listen, acknowledge, build on what someone is saying.	I am calm, I am listening, I am understanding, I am kind.
Self-justification	Accountable	Blame, arguing what I did was right.	Take responsibility.	I am accountable; I am wiling to admit mistakes.
Self-loathing	Nourish	Incessant negative self-talk.	Listen for negative self-judgement thoughts and say No, then affirm...	I am worthy, I open and receptive to. receiving love and kindness, I am loved.
Self-pity	Self-forgetful	Isolate. "No one understands me, nobody cares."	Reach out to others and ask about them.	I am understood, I am loved, I am loving, I am understanding.
Self-reliance	Accept Help	Do it myself, criticize. "I don't need anybody."	Ask for and accept help.	I am open and receptive to receiving help, I am supported.
Self-righteousness	Open-minded	Disagree, argue, dismissive. "I'm right."	Listen, seek to understand another's perspective.	I am open-minded, I am accepting, I am learning, I am understanding.
Self-seeking	Interest in others	Constantly seeking reassurance/approval. "Did you see what I did?" "Do you love me?"	Give attention to and praise others.	I am enough, I am kind.
Anger	Calm	Criticize, say inappropriate things, yell.	Pause. Breathe. Restraint.	I am centered, I am calm, I am kind.

© 2025 Tracy Doyle

Trait	Opposite	Trait Behavior	Opposite	Affirm
Demanding	Accepting	I want what I want when I want it, pressure and impatient with others.	Go with the Flow.	I am centered, I am calm, I am accepting limitations, I am patient.
Dishonest	Honest	Lie by omission "he/she will be upset if they know."	Speak my truth kindly.	I am safe, I am truthful.
Doubt	Trust	Negative self-talk. Believe I'm not capable. "I can't do this."	Redirect.	I am trusting, I am capable, I can.
Envy	Gratitude	Compare; want what others have.	Put down the straw.	I am enough, I am grateful for...
Fear	Trust	Loss = Feeling unsafe Less= Doubt Never= Angry	Redirect.	I am safe, I am calm, I am trusting all is well.
Gossip	Discrete	Talk negatively about others when I feel threatened or unhappy.	Refrain, speak with integrity.	I am kind, I am understanding; I am releasing the need to talk about others.
Impatient	Acceptance	Get frustrated when things don't go the way I want, get short.	Accept things as they are; go with the flow.	I am accepting, I am calm, the way is open the path is clear.
Indecisive	Decisive	Don't commit, avoid, change my mind.	Do what I say and say what I mean.	I am confident; I trust myself to make decisions, I am capable.

© 2025 Tracy Doyle

The Connection Builder

Instructions: Review your *Self-Assessment* and *Life Storm Navigator* to identify hurtful behaviors.

1. Who did you hurt?
2. How did you hurt them? What did you do or not do?
3. What esteemable act can you do to repair the hurt?
4. How will you do this?

Who?	How was I hurtful or unkind?	What esteemable act can I do?	How will I do this?

© 2025 Tracy Doyle

Connection Priorities

Instructions: Review your *Connection Builder*

1. Who in your life are you ready to improve relationships with? Note their names in the **Immediate** column.
2. Who is important to you, but you're not quite ready to improve your relationship with them in the near term? Note their names in the **Later** column.
3. Who in your life have you chosen not to re-engage with? Note their names in the **Never** column.
4. Who in your life do you wish you could have improved relationships with before they passed away? How would you prioritize them if they were here? Add their names to the appropriate column.

Immediate	Later	Never

© 2025 Tracy Doyle

Additional Reading

Butterworth, Eric. Discover the Power Within You: A Guide to the Unexplored Depths Within. Harper One, 2010.

Frankl, Viktor. Man's Search for Meaning. Beacon Press, 2006. (Originally published in 1946.)

Hendrix, Harville. Getting the Love You Want: A Guide for Couples. Macmilan Publishers, 2019. Publishers. (Originally published 1988.)

Jeffers, Susan. Feel the Fear and Do It Anyway: Dynamic Techniques for Turning Fear, Indecision, and Anger into Power, Action, and Love (Revised and Updated). Harvest, 2023.

Maslow, Abraham. Toward a Psychology of Being. Wilder Publications, 2018. (Originally published in 1962.)

McCann, Eileen. The Two Step: The Dance Toward Intimacy. Grove Press. 1985.

Peck, M. Scott. The Road Less Traveled, Timeless Edition: A New Psychology of Love, Traditional Values and Spiritual Growth. Touchstone Books, 1980.

Robbins, Tony. Awaken the Giant Within: How to Take Immediate Control of Your Mental, Emotional, Physical and Financial Destiny! Simon and Schuster, 1992.

Ruiz, Don Miguel. The Four Agreements: A Practical Guide to Personal Freedom. Amber Allen Publishing, 1997.

Singer, Michael A. The Untethered Soul: The Journey Beyond Yourself. New Harbinger Publications, 200.

Strauss, Neil. The Truth: An Uncomfortable Book about Relationships. Dey Street Books, 2015.

Ward, Frances. 52 Weeks of Esteemable Acts: A Guide to Right Living. Hazelden, 2005.

www.ingramcontent.com/pod-product-compliance
Lightning Source LLC
Chambersburg PA
CBHW070050080526
44586CB00013B/989